KU-533-496

HAROLD PINTER
PLAYS THREE

The Homecoming, Tea Party, The Basement, Landscape,
Silence, Night, That's Your Trouble, That's All, Applicant,
Interview, Dialogue for Three, Tea Party (short story), *Old*
Times, No Man's Land.

Harold Pinter was born in London in 1930. He married
Antonia Fraser in 1980. In 1995 he won the David Cohen
British Literature Prize, awarded for a lifetime's achievement
in literature. In 1996 he was given the Laurence Olivier
Award for a lifetime's achievement in theatre. In 2002 he was
made a Companion of Honour for services to literature. In
2005 he received the Wilfred Owen Award for Poetry, the
Franz Kafka Award (Prague) and the Nobel Prize for
Literature. In 2006 he was awarded the Europe Theatre Prize
and in 2007 the highest French honour, the Légion
d'honneur. He died in December 2008.

WITHDRAWN

RECEIVED

3 1 MAR 2009

165285

College of St Mark & St John

165285

HAROLD PINTER

Plays Three

The Homecoming
Tea Party
The Basement
Landscape
Silence
Night
That's Your Trouble
That's All
Applicant
Interview
Dialogue for Three
Tea Party (short story)
Old Times
No Man's Land

faber and faber

This collection first published in 1991
by Faber and Faber Limited
Bloomsbury House
74-77 Great Russell Street
London WC1B 3DA
Reissued in 1996 as *Harold Pinter: Plays Three*
Expanded edition (including *Old Times*
and *No Man's Land*) first published
in 1997

Printed in England by CPI Bookmarque, Croydon

All rights reserved

The Homecoming first published by Methuen & Co. in 1965
Tea Party and *The Basement* first published by Methuen & Co. in 1967
Landscape, *Silence* and *Night* first published by Methuen & Co. in 1969
Applicant first published by Methuen & Co. in 1961
Dialogue for Three first published in Strand vol. 6 no. 3, 1963
That's Your Trouble, *That's All*, *Interview* first published in *The Dwarfs
and eight Review Sketches*, Dramatists Play Service, New York, 1966
'Tea Party' (short story) © first published in Playboy, January 1965
Old Times first published by Methuen & Co. in 1971
No Man's Land first published by Eyre Methuen in 1975, revised in 1975

The Homecoming © H. Pinter Ltd, 1965, 1966, 1967
Tea Party and *The Basement* © H. Pinter Ltd, 1967
Landscape © H. Pinter Ltd, 1968
Silence and *Night* © H. Pinter Ltd, 1969
Applicant © H. Pinter 1961
That's Your Trouble, *That's All*, *Interview* © H. Pinter Ltd, 1966
Dialogue for Three © H. Pinter 1961
'Tea Party' (short story) © H. Pinter and Theatre Promotions Ltd,
1965
Old Times © H. Pinter Ltd, 1971
No Man's Land © H. Pinter Ltd, 1975
Speech at Hamburg (Introduction) © H. Pinter Ltd, 1970

All rights whatsoever in these plays are strictly reserved and applications
to perform them should be made in writing, before rehearsals begin, to
Judy Daish Associates, 2 St Charles Place, London W10 6EG.
The amateur rights for *The Homecoming*, *Landscape*, *Silence* and *Old Times*
are held by Samuel French. Amateur applications for permission to perform
these plays must be made in advance, before rehearsals begin, to
Samuel French Ltd., 52 Fitzroy Street, London W1P 6JR. No performance
may be given unless a licence has first been obtained.

*This book is sold subject to the condition that it shall not, by way of
trade or otherwise, be lent, resold, hired out or otherwise circulated
without the publisher's prior consent in any form of binding or cover
other than that in which it is published and without a similar condition
including this condition being imposed on the subsequent purchaser.*

A CIP record for this book is available from the British Library.

ISBN 978-0-571-19383-7

8 10 9

CONTENTS

INTRODUCTION

A speech made by Harold Pinter in Hamburg, West Germany, on being awarded the 1970 German Shakespeare Prize.

When I was informed that I was to be given this award my reaction was to be startled, even bewildered, while at the same time to feel deeply gratified by this honour. I remain honoured and slightly bewildered, but also frightened. What frightens me is that I have been asked to speak to you today. If I find writing difficult I find giving a public address doubly so.

Once, many years ago, I found myself engaged uneasily in a public discussion on the theatre. Someone asked me what my work was 'about'. I replied with no thought at all and merely to frustrate this line of enquiry: 'The weasel under the cocktail cabinet.' That was a great mistake. Over the years I have seen that remark quoted in a number of learned columns. It has now seemingly acquired a profound significance, and is seen to be a highly relevant and meaningful observation about my own work. But for me the remark meant precisely nothing. Such are the dangers of speaking in public.

In what way can one talk about one's work? I'm a writer, not a critic. When I use the word work I mean work. I regard myself as nothing more than a working man.

I am moved by the fact that the selection committee for the Shakespeare Prize has judged my work, in the context of this award, as worthy of it, but it's impossible for me to understand the reasons that led them to their decision. I'm at the other end of the telescope. The language used, the opinions given, the approvals and objections engendered by one's work happen in a sense outside one's actual experience of it, since the core of that experience consists in writing the stuff. I have a particular relationship with the words I put down on paper and the characters which emerge from them which no one else can share with me. And perhaps that's why I remain bewildered by praise and really quite indifferent to insult. Praise and insult refer to someone called Pinter. I don't know the man they're talking about. I know the plays, but in a totally different way, in a quite private way.

If I am to talk at all I prefer to talk practically about practical matters, but that's no more than a pious hope, since one invariably slips into theorizing, almost without noticing it. And I distrust theory. In whatever capacity I have worked in the theatre, and apart from writing, I have done quite a bit of acting and a certain amount of directing for the stage, I have found that theory, as such, has never been helpful; either to myself, or, I have noticed, to few of my colleagues. The best sort of collaborative working relationship in the theatre, in my view, consists in a kind of stumbling erratic shorthand, through which facts are lost, collided with, fumbled, found again. One excellent director I know has never been known to complete a sentence. He has such instinctive surety and almost subliminal powers of communication that the actors respond to his words before he has said them.

I don't want to imply that I am counselling lack of intelligence as a working aid. On the contrary, I am referring to an intelligence brought to bear on practical and relevant matters, on matters which are active and alive and specific, an intelligence working with others to find the legitimate and therefore compulsory facts and make them concrete for us on the stage. A rehearsal period which consists of philosophical discourse or political treatise does not get the curtain up at eight o'clock.

I have referred to facts, by which I mean theatrical facts. It is true to say that theatrical facts do not easily disclose their secrets, and it is very easy, when they prove stubborn, to distort them, to make them into something else, or to pretend they never existed. This happens more often in the theatre than we care to recognize and is proof either of incompetence or fundamental contempt for the work in hand.

I believe myself that when a writer looks at the blank of the word he has not yet written, or when actors and directors arrive at a given moment on stage, there is only one proper thing that can take place at that moment, and that that thing, that gesture, that word on the page, must alone be found, and once found, scrupulously protected. I think I am talking about necessary shape, both as regards a play and its production.

If there is, as I believe, a necessary, an obligatory shape which a play demands of its writer, then I have never been able to achieve it myself. I have always finished the last draft of a play with a mixture of feelings: relief, disbelief, exhilaration, and a certainty that if I could only wring the play's neck once more it might yield once more to me, that I could get it better, that I could get the better of it, perhaps. But that's impossible. You create the word and in a certain way the word, in finding its own life, stares you out, is obdurate, and more often than not defeats you. You create the characters and they prove to be very tough. They observe you, their writer, warily. It may sound absurd, but I believe I am speaking the truth when I say that I have suffered two kinds of pain through my characters. I have witnessed *their* pain when I am in the act of distorting them, of falsifying them, and I have witnessed their contempt. I have suffered pain when I have been unable to get to the quick of them, when they wilfully elude me, when they withdraw into the shadows. And there's a third and rarer pain. That is when the right word, or the right act jolts them or stills them into their proper life. When that happens the pain is worth having. When that happens I am ready to take them into the nearest bar and buy drinks all round. And I hope they would forgive me my trespasses against them and do the same for me. But there is no question that quite a conflict takes place between the writer and his characters and on the whole I would say the characters are the winners. And that's as it should be, I think. Where a writer sets out a blueprint for his characters, and keeps them rigidly to it, where they do not at any time upset his applecart, where he has mastered them, he has also killed them, or rather terminated their birth, and he has a dead play on his hands.

Sometimes, the director says to me in rehearsal; 'Why does she say this?' I reply: 'Wait a minute, let me look at the text.' I do so, and perhaps I say: 'Doesn't she say this because he said *that*, two pages ago?' Or I say: 'Because that's what she feels.' Or: 'Because she feels something else, and therefore says that.' Or: 'I haven't the faintest idea. But somehow we have to find out.' Sometimes I learn quite a lot from rehearsals.

I have been very fortunate, in my life, in the people I've worked with, and my association with Peter Hall and the Royal Shakespeare Company has, particularly, been greatly satisfying. Peter Hall and I, working together, have found that the image must be pursued with the greatest vigilance, calmly, and once found, must be sharpened, graded, accurately focused and maintained, and that the key word is economy, economy of movement and gesture, of emotion and its expression, both the internal and the external in specific and exact relation to each other, so that there is no wastage and no mess. These are hardly revolutionary conclusions, but I hope no less worthy of restatement for that.

I may appear to be laying too heavy an emphasis on method and technique as opposed to content, but this is not in fact the case. I am not suggesting that the disciplines to which I have been referring be imposed upon the action in terms of a device, or as a formal convenience.

What is made evident before us on the stage can clearly only be made fully evident where the content of the scene has been defined. But I do not understand this definition as one arrived at through the intellect, but a definition made by the actors, using quite a different system. In other words, if I now bring various criteria to bear upon a production, these are not intellectual concepts but facts forged through experience of active participation with good actors and, I hope, a living text.

What am I writing about? Not the weasel under the cocktail cabinet.

I am not concerned with making general statements. I am not interested in theatre used simply as a means of self-expression on the part of the people engaged in it. I find in so much group theatre, under the sweat and assault and noise, nothing but valueless generalizations, naive and quite unfruitful.

I can sum up none of my plays. I can describe none of them, except to say: That is what happened. That is what they said. That is what they did.

I am aware, sometimes, of an insistence in my mind. Images, characters, insisting upon being written. You can pour a drink, make a telephone call or run round the park, and sometimes succeed in suffocating them. You know they're going to make your life hell. But at other times they're unavoidable and you're compelled to try to do them some kind of justice. And while it may be hell, it's certainly for me the best kind of hell to be in.

However, I find it ironic that I have come here to receive this distinguished award as a writer, and that at the moment I am writing nothing and can write nothing. I don't know why. It's a very bad feeling, I know that, but I must say I want more than anything else to fill up a blank page again, and to feel that strange thing happen, birth through fingertips. When you can't write you feel you've been banished from yourself.

THE HOMECOMING

The Homecoming was first presented by the Royal Shakespeare Company at the Aldwych Theatre on 3 June 1965, with the following cast:

MAX, *a man of seventy*	Paul Rogers
LENNY, *a man in his early thirties*	Ian Holm
SAM, *a man of sixty-three*	John Normington
JOEY, *a man in his middle twenties*	Terence Rigby
TEDDY, *a man in his middle thirties*	Michael Bryant
RUTH, *a woman in her early thirties*	Vivien Merchant

Directed by Peter Hall

The Homecoming was revived at the Garrick Theatre in May 1978. The cast was as follows:

MAX	Timothy West
LENNY	Michael Kitchen
SAM	Charles Kay
JOEY	Roger Lloyd Pack
TEDDY	Oliver Cotton
RUTH	Gemma Jones

Directed by Kevin Billington

SUMMER

An old house in North London.

A large room, extending the width of the stage.

The back wall, which contained the door, has been removed. A square arch shape remains. Beyond it, the hall. In the hall a staircase, ascending U.R., well in view. The front door U.R. A coatstand, hooks, etc.

In the room a window, R. Odd tables, chairs. Two large armchairs. A large sofa, L. Against R. wall a large sideboard, the upper half of which contains a mirror. U.L. a radiogram.

Act One

Evening.

LENNY is sitting on the sofa with a newspaper, a pencil in his hand. He wears a dark suit. He makes occasional marks on the back page.

MAX comes in, from the direction of the kitchen. He goes to sideboard, opens top drawer, rummages in it, closes it.

He wears an old cardigan and a cap, and carries a stick.

He walks downstage, stands, looks about the room.

MAX. What have you done with the scissors?

> *Pause.*

I said I'm looking for the scissors. What have you done with them?

> *Pause.*

Did you hear me? I want to cut something out of the paper.

LENNY. I'm reading the paper.

MAX. Not that paper. I haven't even read that paper. I'm talking about last Sunday's paper. I was just having a look at it in the kitchen.

> *Pause.*

Do you hear what I'm saying? I'm talking to you! Where's the scissors?

LENNY (*looking up, quietly*). Why don't you shut up, you daft prat?

> *MAX lifts his stick and points it at him.*

MAX. Don't you talk to me like that. I'm warning you.

He sits in large armchair.

There's an advertisement in the paper about flannel vests. Cut price. Navy surplus. I could do with a few of them.

Pause.

I think I'll have a fag. Give me a fag.

Pause.

I just asked you to give me a cigarette.

Pause.

Look what I'm lumbered with.

He takes a crumpled cigarette from his pocket.

I'm getting old, my word of honour.

He lights it.

You think I wasn't a tearaway? I could have taken care of you, twice over. I'm still strong. You ask your Uncle Sam what I was. But at the same time I always had a kind heart. Always.

Pause.

I used to knock about with a man called MacGregor. I called him Mac. You remember Mac? Eh?

Pause.

Huhh! We were two of the worst hated men in the West End of London. I tell you, I still got the scars. We'd walk into a place, the whole room'd stand up, they'd make way to let us pass. You never heard such silence. Mind you, he was a big man, he was over six foot tall. His family were all MacGregors, they came all the way from Aberdeen, but he was the only one they called Mac.

Pause.

He was very fond of your mother, Mac was. Very fond. He always had a good word for her.

Pause.

Mind you, she wasn't such a bad woman. Even though it made me sick just to look at her rotten stinking face, she wasn't such a bad bitch. I gave her the best bleeding years of my life, anyway.

LENNY. Plug it, will you, you stupid sod, I'm trying to read the paper.

MAX. Listen! I'll chop your spine off, you talk to me like that! You understand? Talking to your lousy filthy father like that!

LENNY. You know what, you're getting demented.

Pause.

What do you think of Second Wind for the three-thirty?

MAX. Where?

LENNY. Sandown Park.

MAX. Don't stand a chance.

LENNY. Sure he does.

MAX. Not a chance.

LENNY. He's the winner.

LENNY *ticks the paper.*

MAX. He talks to me about horses.

Pause.

I used to live on the course. One of the loves of my life. Epsom? I knew it like the back of my hand. I was one of the best-known faces down at the paddock. What a marvellous open-air life.

Pause.

He talks to me about horses. You only read their names in the papers. But I've stroked their manes, I've held them, I've calmed them down before a big race. I was the one they used to call for. Max, they'd say, there's a horse here, he's highly strung, you're the only man on the course who can calm him. It was true. I had a . . . I had an instinctive understanding of animals. I should have been a trainer. Many times I was offered the job – you know, a proper post, by the Duke of . . . I forget his name . . . one of the Dukes. But I had family obligations, my family needed me at home.

Pause.

The times I've watched those animals thundering past the post. What an experience. Mind you, I didn't lose, I made a few bob out of it, and you know why? Because I always had the smell of a good horse. I could smell him. And not only the colts but the fillies. Because the fillies are more highly strung than the colts, they're more unreliable, did you know that? No, what do you know? Nothing. But I was always able to tell a good filly by one particular trick. I'd look her in the eye. You see? I'd stand in front of her and look her straight in the eye, it was a kind of hypnotism, and by the look deep down in her eye I could tell whether she was a stayer or not. It was a gift. I had a gift.

Pause.

And he talks to me about horses.

LENNY. Dad, do you mind if I change the subject?

Pause.

I want to ask you something. The dinner we had before, what was the name of it? What do you call it?

Pause.

Why don't you buy a dog? You're a dog cook. Honest. You think you're cooking for a lot of dogs.

MAX. If you don't like it get out.

LENNY. I am going out. I'm going out to buy myself a proper dinner.

MAX. Well, get out! What are you waiting for?

LENNY *looks at him.*

LENNY. What did you say?

MAX. I said shove off out of it, that's what I said.

LENNY. You'll go before me, Dad, if you talk to me in that tone of voice.

MAX. Will I, you bitch?

MAX *grips his stick.*

LENNY. Oh, Daddy, you're not going to use your stick on me, are you? Eh? Don't use your stick on me Daddy. No, please. It wasn't my fault, it was one of the others. I haven't done anything wrong, Dad, honest. Don't clout me with that stick, Dad.

Silence.

MAX *sits hunched.* LENNY *reads the paper.*

SAM *comes in the front door. He wears a chauffeur's uniform. He hangs his hat on a hook in the hall and comes into the room. He goes to a chair, sits in it and sighs.*

Hullo, Uncle Sam.

SAM. Hullo.

LENNY. How are you, Uncle?

SAM. Not bad. A bit tired.

LENNY. Tired? I bet you're tired. Where you been?

SAM. I've been to London Airport.

LENNY. All the way up to London Airport? What, right up the M4?

SAM. Yes, all the way up there.

LENNY. Tch, tch, tch. Well, I think you're entitled to be tired, Uncle.

SAM. Well, it's the drivers.

LENNY. I know. That's what I'm talking about. I'm talking about the drivers.

SAM. Knocks you out.

Pause.

MAX. I'm here, too, you know.

SAM *looks at him.*

I said I'm here, too. I'm sitting here.

SAM. I know you're here.

Pause.

SAM. I took a Yankee out there today . . . to the Airport.

LENNY. Oh, a Yankee, was it?

SAM. Yes, I been with him all day. Picked him up at the Savoy at half past twelve, took him to the Caprice for his lunch. After lunch I picked him up again, took him down to a house in Eaton Square – he had to pay a visit to a friend there – and then round about tea-time I took him right the way out to the Airport.

LENNY. Had to catch a plane there, did he?

SAM. Yes. Look what he gave me. He gave me a box of cigars.

SAM *takes a box of cigars from his pocket.*

MAX. Come here. Let's have a look at them.

SAM *shows* MAX *the cigars.* MAX *takes one from the box, pinches it and sniffs it.*

It's a fair cigar.

SAM. Want to try one?

MAX *and* SAM *light cigars.*

You know what he said to me? He told me I was the best chauffeur he'd ever had. The best one.

MAX. From what point of view?

SAM. Eh?

MAX. From what point of view?

LENNY. From the point of view of his driving, Dad, and his general sense of courtesy, I should say.

MAX. Thought you were a good driver, did he, Sam? Well, he gave you a first-class cigar.

SAM. Yes, he thought I was the best he'd ever had. They all say that, you know. They won't have anyone else, they only ask for me. They say I'm the best chauffeur in the firm.

LENNY. I bet the other drivers tend to get jealous, don't they, Uncle?

SAM. They do get jealous. They get very jealous.

MAX. Why?

Pause.

SAM. I just told you.

MAX. No, I just can't get it clear, Sam. Why do the other drivers get jealous?

SAM. Because (a) I'm the best driver, and because . . . (b) I don't take liberties.

Pause.

I don't press myself on people, you see. These big business-men, men of affairs, they don't want the driver jawing all the time, they like to sit in the back, have a bit of peace and quiet. After all, they're sitting in a Humber Super Snipe, they can afford to relax. At the same time, though, this is what really makes me special . . . I do know how to pass the time of day when required.

Pause.

For instance, I told this man today I was in the second world war. Not the first. I told him I was too young for the first. But I told him I fought in the second.

Pause.

So did he, it turned out.

LENNY *stands, goes to the mirror and straightens his tie.*

LENNY. He was probably a colonel, or something, in the American Air Force.

SAM. Yes.

LENNY. Probably a navigator, or something like that, in a Flying Fortress. Now he's most likely a high executive in a worldwide group of aeronautical engineers.

SAM. Yes.

LENNY. Yes, I know the kind of man you're talking about.

LENNY *goes out, turning to his right.*

SAM. After all, I'm experienced. I was driving a dust cart at the age of nineteen. Then I was in long-distance haulage. I had ten years as a taxi-driver and I've had five as a private chauffeur.

MAX. It's funny you never got married, isn't it? A man with all your gifts.

Pause.

Isn't it? A man like you?

SAM. There's still time.

MAX. Is there?

Pause.

SAM. You'd be surprised.

MAX. What you been doing, banging away at your lady customers, have you?

SAM. Not me.

MAX. In the back of the Snipe? Been having a few crafty reefs in a layby, have you?

SAM. Not me.

MAX. On the back seat? What about the armrest, was it up or down?

SAM. I've never done that kind of thing in my car.

MAX. Above all that kind of thing, are you, Sam?

SAM. Too true.

MAX. Above having a good bang on the back seat, are you?

SAM. Yes, I leave that to others.

MAX. You leave it to others? What others? You paralysed prat!

SAM. I don't mess up my car! Or my . . . my boss's car! Like other people.

MAX. Other people? What other people?

Pause.

What other people?

Pause.

SAM. Other people.

Pause.

MAX. When you find the right girl, Sam, let your family know, don't forget, we'll give you a number one send-off, I promise you. You can bring her to live here, she can keep us all happy. We'd take it in turns to give her a walk round the park.

SAM. I wouldn't bring her here.

MAX. Sam, it's your decision. You're welcome to bring your bride here, to the place where you live, or on the other hand you can take a suite at the Dorchester. It's entirely up to you.

SAM. I haven't got a bride.

> SAM *stands, goes to the sideboard, takes an apple from the bowl, bites into it.*

Getting a bit peckish.

He looks out of the window.

Never get a bride like you had, anyway. Nothing like your bride . . . going about these days. Like Jessie.

Pause.

After all, I escorted her once or twice, didn't I? Drove her round once or twice in my cab. She was a charming woman.

Pause.

All the same, she was your wife. But still . . . they were some of the most delightful evenings I've ever had. Used to just drive her about. It was my pleasure.

MAX (*softly, closing his eyes*). Christ.

SAM. I used to pull up at a stall and buy her a cup of coffee. She was a very nice companion to be with.

Silence.
JOEY comes in the front door. He walks into the room, takes his jacket off, throws it on a chair and stands.
Silence.

JOEY. Feel a bit hungry.

SAM. Me, too.

MAX. Who do you think I am, your mother? Eh? Honest. They walk in here every time of the day and night like bloody animals. Go and find yourself a mother.

LENNY walks into the room, stands.

JOEY. I've been training down at the gym.

SAM. Yes, the boy's been working all day and training all night.

MAX. What do you want, you bitch? You spend all the day sitting on your arse at London Airport, buy yourself a jamroll. You expect me to sit here waiting to rush into the kitchen the moment you step in the door? You've been living sixty-three years, why don't you learn to cook?

SAM. I can cook.

MAX. Well, go and cook!

Pause.

LENNY. What the boys want, Dad, is your own special brand
of cooking, Dad. That's what the boys look forward to. The
special understanding of food, you know, that you've got.

MAX. Stop calling me Dad. Just stop all that calling me Dad,
do you understand?

LENNY. But I'm your son. You used to tuck me up in bed every
night. He tucked you up, too, didn't he, Joey?

Pause.

He used to like tucking up his sons.

LENNY *turns and goes towards the front door.*

MAX. Lenny.

LENNY (*turning*). What?

MAX. I'll give you a proper tuck up one of these nights, son.
You mark my word.

They look at each other.
LENNY *opens the front door and goes out.*
Silence.

JOEY. I've been training with Bobby Dodd.

Pause.

And I had a good go at the bag as well.

Pause.

I wasn't in bad trim.

MAX. Boxing's a gentleman's game.

Pause.

I'll tell you what you've got to do. What you've got to do is
you've got to learn how to defend yourself, and you've got
to learn how to attack. That's your only trouble as a boxer.
You don't know how to defend yourself, and you don't know
how to attack.

Pause.

Once you've mastered those arts you can go straight to the top.

Pause.

JOEY. I've got a pretty good idea . . . of how to do that.

> JOEY *looks round for his jacket, picks it up, goes out of the*
> *room and up the stairs.*
> *Pause.*

MAX. Sam . . . why don't you go, too, eh? Why don't you just go upstairs? Leave me quiet. Leave me alone.

SAM. I want to make something clear about Jessie, Max. I want to. I do. When I took her out in the cab, round the town, I was taking care of her, for you. I was looking after her for you, when you were busy, wasn't I? I was showing her the West End.

Pause.

You wouldn't have trusted any of your other brothers. You wouldn't have trusted Mac, would you? But you trusted me. I want to remind you.

Pause.

Old Mac died a few years ago, didn't he? Isn't he dead?

Pause.

He was a lousy stinking rotten loudmouth. A bastard uncouth sodding runt. Mind you, he was a good friend of yours.

Pause.

MAX. Eh, Sam . . .
SAM. What?
MAX. Why do I keep you here? You're just an old grub.

SAM. Am I?

MAX. You're a maggot.

SAM. Oh yes?

MAX. As soon as you stop paying your way here, I mean when you're too old to pay your way, you know what I'm going to do? I'm going to give you the boot.

SAM. You are, eh?

MAX. Sure. I mean, bring in the money and I'll put up with you. But when the firm gets rid of you – you can flake off.

SAM. This is my house as well, you know. This was our mother's house.

MAX. One lot after the other. One mess after the other.

SAM. Our father's house.

MAX. Look what I'm lumbered with. One cast-iron bunch of crap after another. One flow of stinking pus after another.

Pause.

Our father! I remember him. Don't worry. You kid yourself. He used to come over to me and look down at me. My old man did. He'd bend right over me, then he'd pick me up. I was only that big. Then he'd dandle me. Give me the bottle. Wipe me clean. Give me a smile. Pat me on the bum. Pass me around, pass me from hand to hand. Toss me up in the air. Catch me coming down. I remember my father.

BLACKOUT.
LIGHTS UP.
Night.
TEDDY *and* RUTH *stand at the threshold of the room.*
They are both well dressed in light summer suits and light raincoats.
Two suitcases are by their side.
They look at the room. TEDDY *tosses the key in his hand, smiles.*

TEDDY. Well, the key worked.

Pause.

They haven't changed the lock.

Pause.

RUTH. No one's here.
TEDDY (*looking up*). They're asleep.

Pause.

RUTH. Can I sit down?
TEDDY. Of course.
RUTH. I'm tired.

Pause.

TEDDY. Then sit down.

She does not move.

That's my father's chair.
RUTH. That one?
TEDDY (*smiling*). Yes, that's it. Shall I go up and see if my room's still there?
RUTH. It can't have moved.
TEDDY. No, I mean if my bed's still there.
RUTH. Someone might be in it.
TEDDY. No. They've got their own beds.

Pause.

RUTH. Shouldn't you wake someone up? Tell them you're here?
TEDDY. Not at this time of night. It's too late.

Pause.

Shall I go up?

He goes into the hall, looks up the stairs, comes back.

Why don't you sit down?

Pause.

I'll just go up . . . have a look.

He goes up the stairs, stealthily.
RUTH *stands, then slowly walks across the room.*
TEDDY *returns.*

It's still there. My room. Empty. The bed's there. What are you doing?

She looks at him.

Blankets, no sheets. I'll find some sheets. I could hear snores. Really. They're all still here, I think. They're all snoring up there. Are you cold?

RUTH. No.

TEDDY. I'll make something to drink, if you like. Something hot.

RUTH. No, I don't want anything.

TEDDY *walks about.*

TEDDY. What do you think of the room? Big, isn't it? It's a big house. I mean, it's a fine room, don't you think? Actually there was a wall, across there . . . with a door. We knocked it down . . . years ago . . . to make an open living area. The structure wasn't affected, you see. My mother was dead.

RUTH *sits.*

Tired?

RUTH. Just a little.

TEDDY. We can go to bed if you like. No point in waking anyone up now. Just go to bed. See them all in the morning . . . see my father in the morning. . . .

Pause.

RUTH. Do you want to stay?

TEDDY. Stay?

Pause.

We've come to stay. We're bound to stay . . . for a few days.
RUTH. I think . . . the children . . . might be missing us.
TEDDY. Don't be silly.
RUTH. They might.
TEDDY. Look, we'll be back in a few days, won't we?

He walks about the room.

Nothing's changed. Still the same.

Pause.

Still, he'll get a surprise in the morning, won't he? The old man. I think you'll like him very much. Honestly. He's a . . . well, he's old, of course. Getting on.

Pause.

I was born here, do you realize that?
RUTH. I know.

Pause.

TEDDY. Why don't you go to bed? I'll find some sheets. I feel . . . wide awake, isn't it odd? I think I'll stay up for a bit. Are you tired?
RUTH. No.
TEDDY. Go to bed. I'll show you the room.
RUTH. No, I don't want to.
TEDDY. You'll be perfectly all right up there without me. Really you will. I mean, I won't be long. Look, it's just up there. It's the first door on the landing. The bathroom's right next door. You . . . need some rest, you know.

Pause.

I just want to . . . walk about for a few minutes. Do you mind?

RUTH. Of course I don't.

TEDDY. Well . . . Shall I show you the room?

RUTH. No, I'm happy at the moment.

TEDDY. You don't have to go to bed. I'm not saying you have to. I mean, you can stay up with me. Perhaps I'll make a cup of tea or something. The only thing is we don't want to make too much noise, we don't want to wake anyone up.

RUTH. I'm not making any noise.

TEDDY. I know you're not.

He goes to her.

(*Gently.*) Look, it's all right, really. I'm here. I mean . . . I'm with you. There's no need to be nervous. Are you nervous?

RUTH. No.

TEDDY. There's no need to be.

Pause.

They're very warm people, really. Very warm. They're my family. They're not ogres.

Pause.

Well, perhaps we should go to bed. After all, we have to be up early, see Dad. Wouldn't be quite right if he found us in bed, I think. (*He chuckles.*) Have to be up before six, come down, say hullo.

Pause.

RUTH. I think I'll have a breath of air.

TEDDY. Air?

Pause.

What do you mean?

RUTH (*standing*). Just a stroll.

TEDDY. At this time of night? But we've . . . only just got here. We've got to go to bed.

RUTH. I just feel like some air.

TEDDY. But I'm going to bed.

RUTH. That's all right.

TEDDY. But what am I going to do?

Pause.

The last thing I want is a breath of air. Why do you want a breath of air?

RUTH. I just do.

TEDDY. But it's late.

RUTH. I won't go far. I'll come back.

Pause.

TEDDY. I'll wait up for you.

RUTH. Why?

TEDDY. I'm not going to bed without you.

RUTH. Can I have the key?

He gives it to her.

Why don't you go to bed?

He puts his arms on her shoulders and kisses her.
They look at each other, briefly. She smiles.

I won't be long.

She goes out of the front door.
TEDDY *goes to the window, peers out after her, half turns from the window, stands, suddenly chews his knuckles.*
LENNY *walks into the room from* U.L. *He stands. He wears pyjamas and dressing-gown. He watches* TEDDY.
TEDDY *turns and sees him.*
Silence.

TEDDY. Hullo, Lenny.

LENNY. Hullo, Teddy.

Pause.

TEDDY. I didn't hear you come down the stairs.

LENNY. I didn't.

Pause.

I sleep down here now. Next door. I've got a kind of study, workroom cum bedroom next door now, you see.

TEDDY. Oh. Did I . . . wake you up?

LENNY. No. I just had an early night tonight. You know how it is. Can't sleep. Keep waking up.

Pause

TEDDY. How are you?

LENNY. Well, just sleeping a bit restlessly, that's all. Tonight, anyway.

TEDDY. Bad dreams?

LENNY. No, I wouldn't say I was dreaming. It's not exactly a dream. It's just that something keeps waking me up. Some kind of tick.

TEDDY. A tick?

LENNY. Yes.

TEDDY. Well, what is it?

LENNY. I don't know.

Pause.

TEDDY. Have you got a clock in your room?

LENNY. Yes.

TEDDY. Well, maybe it's the clock.

LENNY. Yes, could be, I suppose.

Pause.

Well, if it's the clock I'd better do something about it, Stifle it in some way, or something.

Pause.

TEDDY. I've . . . just come back for a few days
LENNY. Oh yes? Have you?

Pause.

TEDDY. How's the old man?
LENNY. He's in the pink.

Pause.

TEDDY. I've been keeping well.
LENNY. Oh, have you?

Pause.

Staying the night then, are you?
TEDDY. Yes.
LENNY. Well, you can sleep in your old room.
TEDDY. Yes, I've been up.
LENNY. Yes, you can sleep there.

LENNY *yawns.*

Oh well.
TEDDY. I'm going to bed.
LENNY. Are you?
TEDDY. Yes, I'll get some sleep.
LENNY. Yes I'm going to bed, too.

TEDDY *picks up the cases.*

I'll give you a hand.
TEDDY. No, they're not heavy.

TEDDY *goes into the hall with the cases.*
LENNY *turns out the light in the room.*
The light in the hall remains on.
LENNY *follows into the hall.*

LENNY. Nothing you want?

TEDDY. Mmmm?

LENNY. Nothing you might want, for the night? Glass of water, anything like that?

TEDDY. Any sheets anywhere?

LENNY. In the sideboard in your room.

TEDDY. Oh, good.

LENNY. Friends of mine occasionally stay there, you know, in your room, when they're passing through this part of the world.

> LENNY *turns out the hall light and turns on the first landing light.*
>
> TEDDY *begins to walk up the stairs.*

TEDDY. Well, I'll see you at breakfast, then.

LENNY. Yes, that's it. Ta-ta.

> TEDDY *goes upstairs.*
> LENNY *goes off* L.
> *Silence.*
> *The landing light goes out.*
> *Slight night light in the hall and room.*
> LENNY *comes back into the room, goes to the window and looks out.*
> *He leaves the window and turns on a lamp.*
> *He is holding a small clock.*
> *He sits, places the clock in front of him, lights a cigarette and sits.*
> RUTH *comes in the front door.*
> *She stands still.* LENNY *turns his head, smiles. She walks slowly into the room.*

LENNY. Good evening.

RUTH. Morning, I think.

LENNY. You're right there.

> *Pause.*

My name's Lenny. What's yours?

RUTH. Ruth.

She sits, puts her coat collar around her.

LENNY. Cold?
RUTH. No.
LENNY. It's been a wonderful summer, hasn't it? Remarkable.

Pause.

Would you like something? Refreshment of some kind? An aperitif, anything like that?
RUTH. No, thanks.
LENNY. I'm glad you said that. We haven't got a drink in the house. Mind you, I'd soon get some in, if we had a party or something like that. Some kind of celebration . . . you know.

Pause.

You must be connected with my brother in some way. The one who's been abroad.
RUTH. I'm his wife.
LENNY. Eh listen, I wonder if you can advise me. I've been having a bit of a rough time with this clock. The tick's been keeping me up. The trouble is I'm not all that convinced it was the clock. I mean there are lots of things which tick in the night, don't you find that? All sorts of objects, which, in the day, you wouldn't call anything else but commonplace. They give you no trouble. But in the night any given one of a number of them is liable to start letting out a bit of a tick. Whereas you look at these objects in the day and they're just commonplace. They're as quiet as mice during the daytime. So . . . all things being equal . . . this question of me saying it was the clock that woke me up, well, that could very easily prove something of a false hypothesis.

He goes to the sideboard, pours from a jug into a glass, takes the glass to RUTH.

Here you are. I bet you could do with this.

RUTH. What is it?

LENNY. Water.

She takes it, sips, places the glass on a small table by her chair.

LENNY *watches her.*

Isn't it funny? I've got my pyjamas on and you're fully dressed.

He goes to the sideboard and pours another glass of water.

Mind if I have one? Yes, it's funny seeing my old brother again after all these years. It's just the sort of tonic my Dad needs, you know. He'll be chuffed to his bollocks in the morning, when he sees his eldest son. I was surprised myself when I saw Teddy, you know. Old Ted. I thought he was in America.

RUTH. We're on a visit to Europe.

LENNY. What, both of you?

RUTH. Yes.

LENNY. What, you sort of live with him over there, do you?

RUTH. We're married.

LENNY. On a visit to Europe, eh? Seen much of it?

RUTH. We've just come from Italy.

LENNY. Oh, you went to Italy first, did you? And then he brought you over here to meet the family, did he? Well, the old man'll be pleased to see you, I can tell you.

RUTH. Good.

LENNY. What did you say?

RUTH. Good.

Pause.

LENNY. Where'd you go to in Italy?

RUTH. Venice.

LENNY. Not dear old Venice? Eh? That's funny. You know, I've always had a feeling that if I'd been a soldier in the last war – say in the Italian campaign – I'd probably have found myself in Venice. I've always had that feeling. The trouble was I was too young to serve, you see. I was only a child, I was too small, otherwise I've got a pretty shrewd idea I'd probably have gone through Venice. Yes, I'd almost certainly have gone through it with my battalion. Do you mind if I hold your hand?

RUTH. Why?

LENNY. Just a touch.

He stands and goes to her.

Just a tickle.

RUTH. Why?

He looks down at her.

LENNY. I'll tell you why.

Slight pause.

One night, not too long ago, one night down by the docks, I was standing alone under an arch, watching all the men jibbing the boom, out in the harbour, and playing about with a yardarm, when a certain lady came up to me and made me a certain proposal. This lady had been searching for me for days. She'd lost tracks of my whereabouts. However, the fact was she eventually caught up with me, and when she caught up with me she made me this certain proposal. Well, this proposal wasn't entirely out of order and normally I would have subscribed to it. I mean I would have subscribed to it in the normal course of events. The only trouble was she was falling apart with the pox. So I turned it down. Well, this lady was very insistent and started taking liberties with me down under this arch, liberties which by any criterion I couldn't be expected to tolerate, the facts being what they were, so I clumped her one. It was on my mind at the time to do away with her, you know, to kill her, and the fact is, that as killings go, it would have been a simple matter, nothing to it. Her chauffeur, who had located me for her, he'd popped round the corner to have a drink, which just left this lady and myself, you see, alone, standing underneath this arch, watching all the steamers steaming up, no one about, all quiet on the Western Front, and there she was up against this wall – well, just sliding down the wall, following the blow I'd given her. Well, to sum up, everything was in my favour, for a killing. Don't worry about the chauffeur. The chauffeur would never have spoken. He was an old friend of the family. But . . . in the end I thought . . . Aaah, why go to all the bother . . . you know, getting rid of the corpse and all that, getting yourself into a state of tension. So I just gave her another belt in the nose and a couple of turns of the boot and sort of left it at that.

RUTH. How did you know she was diseased?

LENNY. How did I know?

Pause.

I decided she was.

Silence.

You and my brother are newly-weds, are you?

RUTH. We've been married six years.

LENNY. He's always been my favourite brother, old Teddy. Do you know that? And my goodness we are proud of him here, I can tell you. Doctor of Philosophy and all that . . . leaves quite an impression. Of course, he's a very sensitive man, isn't he? Ted. Very. I've often wished I was as sensitive as he is.

RUTH. Have you?

LENNY. Oh yes. Oh yes, very much so. I mean, I'm not
saying I'm not sensitive. I am. I could just be a bit more so,
that's all.

RUTH. Could you?

LENNY. Yes, just a bit more so, that's all.

Pause.

I mean, I am very sensitive to atmosphere, but I tend to get
desensitized, if you know what I mean, when people make
unreasonable demands on me. For instance, last Christmas
I decided to do a bit of snow-clearing for the Borough
Council, because we had a heavy snow over here that year
in Europe. I didn't have to do this snow-clearing – I mean
I wasn't financially embarrassed in any way – it just appealed
to me, it appealed to something inside me. What I antici-
pated with a good deal of pleasure was the brisk cold bite
in the air in the early morning. And I was right. I had to get
my snowboots on and I had to stand on a corner, at about
five-thirty in the morning, to wait for the lorry to pick me
up, to take me to the allotted area. Bloody freezing. Well,
the lorry came, I jumped on the tailboard, headlights on,
dipped, and off we went. Got there, shovels up, fags on,
and off we went, deep into the December snow, hours before
cockcrow. Well, that morning, while I was having my mid-
morning cup of tea in a neighbouring cafe, the shovel
standing by my chair, an old lady approached me and asked
me if I would give her a hand with her iron mangle. Her
brother-in-law, she said, had left it for her, but he'd left it
in the wrong room, he'd left it in the front room. Well,
naturally, she wanted it in the back room. It was a present
he'd given her, you see, a mangle, to iron out the washing.
But he'd left it in the wrong room, he'd left it in the front
room, well that was a silly place to leave it, it couldn't stay
there. So I took time off to give her a hand. She only lived
up the road. Well, the only trouble was when I got there I

couldn't move this mangle. It must have weighed about half a ton. How this brother-in-law got it up there in the first place I can't even begin to envisage. So there I was, doing a bit of shoulders on with the mangle, risking a rupture, and this old lady just standing there, waving me on, not even lifting a little finger to give me a helping hand. So after a few minutes I said to her, now look here, why don't you stuff this iron mangle up your arse? Anyway, I said, they're out of date, you want to get a spin drier. I had a good mind to give her a workover there and then, but as I was feeling jubilant with the snow-clearing I just gave her a short-arm jab to the belly and jumped on a bus outside. Excuse me, shall I take this ashtray out of your way?

RUTH. It's not in my way.

LENNY. It seems to be in the way of your glass. The glass was about to fall. Or the ashtray. I'm rather worried about the carpet. It's not me, it's my father. He's obsessed with order and clarity. He doesn't like mess. So, as I don't believe you're smoking at the moment, I'm sure you won't object if I move the ashtray.

He does so.

And now perhaps I'll relieve you of your glass.

RUTH. I haven't quite finished.

LENNY. You've consumed quite enough, in my opinion.

RUTH. No, I haven't.

LENNY. Quite sufficient, in my own opinion.

RUTH. Not in mine, Leonard.

Pause.

LENNY. Don't call me that, please.

RUTH. Why not?

LENNY. That's the name my mother gave me.

Pause.

Just give me the glass.

RUTH. No.

Pause.

LENNY. I'll take it, then.

RUTH. If you take the glass . . . I'll take you.

Pause.

LENNY. How about me taking the glass without you taking me?

RUTH. Why don't I just take you?

Pause.

LENNY. You're joking.

Pause.

You're in love, anyway, with another man. You've had a secret liaison with another man. His family didn't even know. Then you come here without a word of warning and start to make trouble.

She picks up the glass and lifts it towards him.

RUTH. Have a sip. Go on. Have a sip from my glass.

He is still.

Sit on my lap. Take a long cool sip.

She pats her lap. Pause.
She stands, moves to him with the glass.

Put your head back and open your mouth.

LENNY. Take that glass away from me.

RUTH. Lie on the floor. Go on. I'll pour it down your throat.

LENNY. What are you doing, making me some kind of proposal?

She laughs shortly, drains the glass.

RUTH. Oh, I was thirsty.

> *She smiles at him, puts the glass down, goes into the hall and up the stairs.*
> *He follows into the hall and shouts up the stairs.*

LENNY. What was that supposed to be? Some kind of proposal?

> *Silence.*
> *He comes back into the room, goes to his own glass, drains it.*
> *A door slams upstairs.*
> *The landing light goes on.*
> MAX *comes down the stairs, in pyjamas and cap. He comes into the room.*

MAX. What's going on here? You drunk?

> *He stares at* LENNY.

What are you shouting about? You gone mad?

> LENNY *pours another glass of water.*

Prancing about in the middle of the night shouting your head off. What are you, a raving lunatic?

LENNY. I was thinking aloud.

MAX. Is Joey down here? You been shouting at Joey?

LENNY. Didn't you hear what I said, Dad? I said I was thinking aloud.

MAX. You were thinking so loud you got me out of bed.

LENNY. Look, why don't you just . . . pop off, eh?

MAX. Pop off? He wakes me up in the middle of the night, I think we got burglars here, I think he's got a knife stuck in him, I come down here, he tells me to pop off.

> LENNY *sits down.*

He was talking to someone. Who could he have been talking to? They're all asleep. He was having a conversation with someone. He won't tell me who it was. He pretends he was thinking aloud. What are you doing, hiding someone here?

LENNY. I was sleepwalking. Get out of it, leave me alone, will you?

MAX. I want an explanation, you understand? I asked you who you got hiding here.

   Pause.

LENNY. I'll tell you what, Dad, since you're in the mood for a bit of a . . . chat, I'll ask you a question. It's a question I've been meaning to ask you for some time. That night . . . you know . . . the night you got me . . . that night with Mum, what was it like? Eh? When I was just a glint in your eye. What was it like? What was the background to it? I mean, I want to know the real facts about my background. I mean, for instance, is it a fact that you had me in mind all the time, or is it a fact that I was the last thing you had in mind?

   Pause.

I'm only asking this in a spirit of inquiry, you understand that, don't you? I'm curious. And there's lots of people of my age share that curiosity, you know that, Dad? They often ruminate, sometimes singly, sometimes in groups, about the true facts of that particular night – the night they were made in the image of those two people *at it*. It's a question long overdue, from my point of view, but as we happen to be passing the time of day here tonight I thought I'd pop it to you.

   Pause.

MAX. You'll drown in your own blood.

LENNY. If you prefer to answer the question in writing I've got no objection.

   MAX *stands.*

I should have asked my dear mother. Why didn't I ask my dear mother? Now it's too late. She's passed over to the other side.

> MAX *spits at him.*
> LENNY *looks down at the carpet.*

Now look what you've done. I'll have to Hoover that in the morning, you know.

> MAX *turns and walks up the stairs.*
> LENNY *sits still.*
> BLACKOUT.
> LIGHTS UP.

> *Morning.*
> JOEY *in front of the mirror. He is doing some slow limbering-up exercises. He stops, combs his hair, carefully. He then shadowboxes, heavily, watching himself in the mirror.*
> MAX *comes in from* U.L.
> *Both* MAX *and* JOEY *are dressed.* MAX *watches* JOEY *in silence.* JOEY *stops shadowboxing, picks up a newspaper and sits.*
> *Silence.*

MAX. I hate this room.

> *Pause.*

It's the kitchen I like. It's nice in there. It's cosy.

> *Pause.*

But I can't stay in there. You know why? Because he's always washing up in there, scraping the plates, driving me out of the kitchen, that's why.

JOEY. Why don't you bring your tea in here?

MAX. I don't want to bring my tea in here. I hate it here. I want to drink my tea in there.

He goes into the hall and looks towards the kitchen.

What's he doing in there?

He returns.

What's the time?

JOEY. Half past six.

MAX. Half past six.

Pause.

I'm going to see a game of football this afternoon. You want to come?

Pause.

I'm talking to you.

JOEY. I'm training this afternoon. I'm doing six rounds with Blackie.

MAX. That's not till five o'clock. You've got time to see a game of football before five o'clock. It's the first game of the season.

JOEY. No, I'm not going.

MAX. Why not?

Pause.

MAX *goes into the hall.*

Sam! Come here!

MAX comes back into the room.
SAM enters with a cloth.

SAM. What?

MAX. What are you doing in there?

SAM. Washing up.

MAX. What else?

SAM. Getting rid of your leavings.

MAX. Putting them in the bin, eh?

SAM. Right in.

MAX. What point you trying to prove?

SAM. No point.

MAX. Oh yes, you are. You resent making my breakfast, that's what it is, isn't it? That's why you bang round the kitchen like that, scraping the frying-pan, scraping all the leavings into the bin, scraping all the plates, scraping all the tea out of the teapot . . . that's why you do that, every single stinking morning. I know. Listen, Sam. I want to say something to you. From my heart.

He moves closer.

I want you to get rid of these feelings of resentment you've got towards me. I wish I could understand them. Honestly, have I ever given you cause? Never. When Dad died he said to me, Max, look after your brothers. That's exactly what he said to me.

SAM. How could he say that when he was dead?

MAX. What?

SAM. How could he speak if he was dead?

Pause.

MAX. Before he died, Sam. Just before. They were his last words. His last sacred words, Sammy. You think I'm joking? You think when my father spoke – on his death-bed – I wouldn't obey his words to the last letter? You hear that, Joey? He'll stop at nothing. He's even prepared to spit on the memory of our Dad. What kind of a son were you, you wet wick? You spent half your time doing crossword puzzles! We took you into the butcher's shop, you couldn't even sweep the dust off the floor. We took MacGregor into the shop, he could run the place by the end of a week. Well, I'll tell you one thing. I respected my father not only as a man but as a number one butcher! And to prove it I followed him into the shop. I learned to carve a carcass at his knee. I commemorated his name in blood. I gave birth to three grown men! All on my own bat. What have you done?

Pause.

What have you done? You tit!

SAM. Do you want to finish the washing up? Look, here's the cloth.

MAX. So try to get rid of these feelings of resentment, Sam. After all, we are brothers.

SAM. Do you want the cloth? Here you are. Take it.

> TEDDY *and* RUTH *come down the stairs. They walk across the hall and stop just inside the room.*
> *The others turn and look at them.* JOEY *stands.*
> TEDDY *and* RUTH *are wearing dressing-gowns.*
> *Silence.*
> TEDDY *smiles.*

TEDDY. Hullo . . . Dad . . . We overslept.

Pause.

What's for breakfast?

> *Silence.*
> TEDDY *chuckles.*

Huh. We overslept.

> MAX *turns to* SAM.

MAX. Did you know he was here?

SAM. No.

> MAX *turns to* JOEY.

MAX. Did you know he was here?

Pause.

I asked you if you knew he was here.

JOEY. No.

MAX. Then who knew?

Pause.

Who knew?

Pause.

I didn't know.

TEDDY. I was going to come down, Dad, I was going to . . . be here, when you came down.

Pause.

How are you?

Pause.

Uh . . . look, I'd . . . like you to meet . . .

MAX. How long you been in this house?

TEDDY. All night.

MAX. All night? I'm a laughing-stock. How did you get in?

TEDDY. I had my key.

MAX whistles and laughs.

MAX. Who's this?

TEDDY. I was just going to introduce you.

MAX. Who asked you to bring tarts in here?

TEDDY. Tarts?

MAX. Who asked you to bring dirty tarts into this house?

TEDDY. Listen, don't be silly –

MAX. You been here all night?

TEDDY. Yes, we arrived from Venice –

MAX. We've had a smelly scrubber in my house all night. We've had a stinking pox-ridden slut in my house all night.

TEDDY. Stop it! What are you talking about?

MAX. I haven't seen the bitch for six years, he comes home without a word, he brings a filthy scrubber off the street, he shacks up in my house!

TEDDY. She's my wife! We're married!

Pause.

MAX. I've never had a whore under this roof before. Ever since your mother died. My word of honour. (*To* JOEY.) Have you ever had a whore here? Has Lenny ever had a whore here? They come back from America, they bring the slopbucket with them. They bring the bedpan with them. (*To* TEDDY.) Take that disease away from me. Get her away from me.

TEDDY. She's my wife.

MAX (*to* JOEY). Chuck them out.

Pause.

A Doctor of Philosophy, Sam, you want to meet a Doctor of Philosophy? (*To* JOEY.) I said chuck them out.

Pause.

What's the matter? You deaf?

JOEY. You're an old man. (*To* TEDDY.) He's an old man.

> LENNY *walks into the room, in a dressing-gown.*
> *He stops.*
> *They all look round.*
> MAX *turns back, hits* JOEY *in the stomach with all his might.*
> JOEY *contorts, staggers across the stage.* MAX, *with the exertion of the blow, begins to collapse. His knees buckle. He clutches his stick.*
> SAM *moves forward to help him.*
> MAX *hits him across the head with his stick,* SAM *sits, head in hands.*

JOEY, *hands pressed to his stomach, sinks down at the feet of*
RUTH
She looks down at him.
LENNY *and* TEDDY *are still.*
JOEY *slowly stands. He is close to* RUTH. *He turns from*
RUTH, *looks round at* MAX.
SAM *clutches his head.*
MAX *breathes heavily, very slowly gets to his feet.*
JOEY *moves to him.*
They look at each other.
Silence.
MAX *moves past* JOEY, *walks towards* RUTH. *He gestures
with his stick.*

MAX. Miss.

RUTH *walks towards him.*

RUTH. Yes?

He looks at her.

MAX. You a mother?
RUTH. Yes.
MAX. How many you got?
RUTH. Three.

He turns to TEDDY.

MAX. All yours, Ted?

Pause.

Teddy, why don't we have a nice cuddle and kiss, eh? Like
the old days? What about a nice cuddle and kiss, eh?
TEDDY. Come on, then.

Pause.

MAX. You want to kiss your old father? Want a cuddle with
your old father?

TEDDY. Come on, then.

> TEDDY *moves a step towards him.*

Come on.

> *Pause.*

MAX. You still love your old Dad, eh?

> *They face each other.*

TEDDY. Come on, Dad. I'm ready for the cuddle.

> MAX *begins to chuckle, gurgling.*
> *He turns to the family and addresses them.*

MAX. He still loves his father!

Curtain

Act Two

Afternoon.

MAX, TEDDY, LENNY *and* SAM *are about the stage, lighting cigars.*

JOEY *comes in from* U.L. *with a coffee tray, followed by* RUTH. *He puts the tray down.* RUTH *hands coffee to all the men. She sits with her cup.* MAX *smiles at her.*

RUTH. That was a very good lunch.

MAX. I'm glad you liked it. (*To the others.*) Did you hear that? (*To* RUTH.) Well, I put my heart and soul into it, I can tell you. (*He sips.*) And this is a lovely cup of coffee.

RUTH. I'm glad.

    Pause.

MAX. I've got the feeling you're a first-rate cook.

RUTH. I'm not bad.

MAX. No, I've got the feeling you're a number one cook. Am I right, Teddy?

TEDDY. Yes, she's a very good cook.

    Pause.

MAX. Well, it's a long time since the whole family was together, eh? If only your mother was alive. Eh, what do you say, Sam? What would Jessie say if she was alive? Sitting here with her three sons. Three fine grown-up lads. And a lovely daughter-in-law. The only shame is her grandchildren aren't here. She'd have petted them and cooed over them, wouldn't she, Sam? She'd have fussed over them and played with them, told them stories, tickled them – I tell you she'd have been hysterical. (*To* RUTH.) Mind you, she taught those boys everything they know. She taught them

all the morality they know. I'm telling you. Every single bit
of the moral code they live by – was taught to them by their
mother. And she had a heart to go with it. What a heart. Eh,
Sam? Listen, what's the use of beating round the bush?
That woman was the backbone to this family. I mean, I was
busy working twenty-four hours a day in the shop, I was
going all over the country to find meat, I was making my
way in the world, but I left a woman at home with a will of
iron, a heart of gold and a mind. Right, Sam?

Pause.

What a mind.

Pause.

Mind you, I was a generous man to her. I never left her
short of a few bob. I remember one year I entered into
negotiations with a top-class group of butchers with conti-
nental connections. I was going into association with them.
I remember the night I came home, I kept quiet. First of all
I gave Lenny a bath, then Teddy a bath, then Joey a bath.
What fun we used to have in the bath, eh, boys? Then I
came downstairs and I made Jessie put her feet up on a
pouffe – what happened to that pouffe, I haven't seen it for
years – she put her feet up on the pouffe and I said to her,
Jessie, I think our ship is going to come home, I'm going to
treat you to a couple of items, I'm going to buy you a dress in
pale corded blue silk, heavily encrusted in pearls, and for
casual wear, a pair of pantaloons in lilac flowered taffeta.
Then I gave her a drop of cherry brandy. I remember the
boys came down, in their pyjamas, all their hair shining,
their faces pink, it was before they started shaving, and they
knelt down at our feet, Jessie's and mine. I tell you, it was
like Christmas.

Pause.

RUTH. What happened to the group of butchers?

MAX. The group? They turned out to be a bunch of criminals like everyone else.

Pause.

This is a lousy cigar.

He stubs it out.

He turns to SAM.

What time you going to work?

SAM. Soon.

MAX. You've got a job on this afternoon, haven't you?

SAM. Yes, I know.

MAX. What do you mean, you know? You'll be late. You'll lose your job. What are you trying to do, humiliate me?

SAM. Don't worry about me.

MAX. It makes the bile come up in my mouth. The bile – you understand? (*To* RUTH.) I worked as a butcher all my life, using the chopper and the slab, the slab, you know what I mean, the chopper and the slab! To keep my family in luxury. Two families! My mother was bedridden, my brothers were all invalids. I had to earn the money for the leading psychiatrists. I had to read books! I had to study the disease, so that I could cope with an emergency at every stage. A crippled family, three bastard sons, a slutbitch of a wife – don't talk to me about the pain of childbirth – I suffered the pain, I've still got the pangs – when I give a little cough my back collapses – and here I've got a lazy idle bugger of a brother won't even get to work on time. The best chauffeur in the world. All his life he's sat in the front seat giving lovely hand signals. You call that work? This man doesn't know his gearbox from his arse!

SAM. You go and ask my customers! I'm the only one they ever ask for.

MAX. What do the other drivers do, sleep all day?

SAM. I can only drive one car. They can't all have me at the same time.

MAX. Anyone could have you at the same time. You'd bend over for half a dollar on Blackfriars Bridge.

SAM. Me!

MAX. For two bob and a toffee apple.

SAM. He's insulting me. He's insulting his brother. I'm driving a man to Hampton Court at four forty-five.

MAX. Do you want to know who could drive? MacGregor! MacGregor was a driver.

SAM. Don't you believe it.

> MAX *points his stick at* SAM.

MAX. He didn't even fight in the war. This man didn't even fight in the bloody war!

SAM. I did!

MAX. Who did you kill?

> *Silence.*
> SAM *gets up, goes to* RUTH, *shakes her hand and goes out of the front door.*
> MAX *turns to* TEDDY.

Well, how you been keeping, son?

TEDDY. I've been keeping very well, Dad.

MAX. It's nice to have you with us, son.

TEDDY. It's nice to be back, Dad.

> *Pause.*

MAX. You should have told me you were married, Teddy. I'd have sent you a present. Where was the wedding, in America?

TEDDY. No, Here. The day before we left.

MAX. Did you have a big function?

TEDDY. No, there was no one there.

MAX. You're mad. I'd have given you a white wedding. We'd

have had the cream of the cream here. I'd have been only
too glad to bear the expense, my word of honour.

Pause.

TEDDY. You were busy at the time. I didn't want to bother
you.
MAX. But you're my own flesh and blood. You're my first born.
I'd have dropped everything. Sam would have driven you
to the reception in the Snipe, Lenny would have been your
best man, and then we'd have all seen you off on the boat. I
mean, you don't think I disapprove of marriage, do you?
Don't be daft. (*To* RUTH.) I've been begging my two
youngsters for years to find a nice feminine girl with proper
credentials – it makes life worth living. (*To* TEDDY.) Anyway, what's the difference, you did it, you made a wonderful
choice, you've got a wonderful family, a marvellous career
. . . so why don't we let bygones by bygones?

Pause.

You know what I'm saying? I want you both to know that
you have my blessing.
TEDDY. Thank you.
MAX. Don't mention it. How many other houses in the district
have got a Doctor of Philosophy sitting down drinking a cup
of coffee?

Pause.

RUTH. I'm sure Teddy's very happy . . . to know that you're
pleased with me.

Pause.

I think he wondered whether you would be pleased with me.
MAX. But you're a charming woman.

Pause.

RUTH. I was . . .
MAX. What?

Pause.

What she say?

They all look at her.

RUTH. I was . . . different . . . when I met Teddy . . .
first.
TEDDY. No you weren't. You were the same.
RUTH. I wasn't.
MAX. Who cares? Listen, live in the present, what are you
worrying about? I mean, don't forget the earth's about
five thousand million years old, at least. Who can afford to
live in the past?

Pause.

TEDDY. She's a great help to me over there. She's a wonderful
wife and mother. She's a very popular woman. She's got
lots of friends. It's a great life, at the University . . . you
know . . . it's a very good life. We've got a lovely house
. . . we've got all . . . we've got everything we want. It's
a very stimulating environment.

Pause.

My department . . . is highly successful.

Pause.

We've got three boys, you know.
MAX. All boys? Isn't that funny, eh? You've got three, I've
got three. You've got three nephews, Joey. Joey! You're
an uncle, do you hear? You could teach them how to
box.

Pause.

JOEY (*to* RUTH). I'm a boxer. In the evenings, after work. I'm in demolition in the daytime.

RUTH. Oh?

JOEY. Yes. I hope to be full time, when I get more bouts.

MAX (*to* LENNY). He speaks so easily to his sister-in-law, do you notice? That's because she's an intelligent and sympathetic woman.

He leans to her.

Eh, tell me, do you think the children are missing their mother?

She looks at him.

TEDDY. Of course they are. They love her. We'll be seeing them soon.

Pause.

LENNY (*to* TEDDY). Your cigar's gone out.

TEDDY. Oh, yes.

LENNY. Want a light?

TEDDY. No. No.

Pause.

So has yours.

LENNY. Oh, yes.

Pause.

Eh, Teddy, you haven't told us much about your Doctorship of Philosophy. What do you teach?

TEDDY. Philosophy.

LENNY. Well, I want to ask you something. Do you detect a certain logical incoherence in the central affirmations of Christian theism?

TEDDY. That question doesn't fall within my province.

LENNY. Well, look at it this way . . . you don't mind my asking you some questions, do you?

TEDDY. If they're within my province.

LENNY. Well, look at it this way. How can the unknown merit reverence? In other words, how can you revere that of which you're ignorant? At the same time, it would be ridiculous to propose that what we *know* merits reverence. What we know merits any one of a number of things, but it stands to reason reverence isn't one of them. In other words, apart from the known and the unknown, what else is there?

Pause.

TEDDY. I'm afraid I'm the wrong person to ask.

LENNY. But you're a philosopher. Come on, be frank. What do you make of all this business of being and not-being?

TEDDY. What do you make of it?

LENNY. Well, for instance, take a table. Philosophically speaking. What is it?

TEDDY. A table.

LENNY. Ah. You mean it's nothing else but a table. Well, some people would envy your certainty, wouldn't they, Joey? For instance, I've got a couple of friends of mine, we often sit round the Ritz Bar having a few liqueurs, and they're always saying things like that, you know, things like: Take a table, take it. All right, I say, *take* it, *take* a table, but once you've taken it, what you going to do with it? Once you've got hold of it, where you going to take it?

MAX. You'd probably sell it.

LENNY. You wouldn't get much for it.

JOEY. Chop it up for firewood.

LENNY *looks at him and laughs.*

RUTH. Don't be too sure though. You've forgotten something. Look at me. I . . . move my leg. That's all it is. But I

wear . . . underwear . . . which moves with me . . . it
. . . captures your attention. Perhaps you misinterpret. The
action is simple. It's a leg . . . moving. My lips move.
Why don't you restrict . . . your observations to that?
Perhaps the fact that they move is more significant . . .
than the words which come through them. You must bear
that . . . possibility . . . in mind.

> *Silence*
> TEDDY *stands.*

I was born quite near here.

> *Pause.*

Then . . . six years ago, I went to America.

> *Pause.*

It's all rock. And sand. It stretches . . . so far . . . everywhere you look. And there's lots of insects there.

> *Pause.*

And there's lots of insects there.

> *Silence.*
> *She is still.*
> MAX *stands.*

MAX. Well, it's time to go to the gym. Time for your workout,
Joey.

LENNY (*standing*). I'll come with you.

> JOEY *sits looking at* RUTH.

MAX. Joe.

> JOEY *stands. The three go out.*
> TEDDY *sits by* RUTH, *holds her hand.*
> *She smiles at him.*
> *Pause.*

TEDDY. I think we'll go back. Mmnn?

Pause.

Shall we go home?

RUTH. Why?

TEDDY. Well, we were only here for a few days, weren't we?
We might as well . . . cut it short, I think.

RUTH. Why? Don't you like it here?

TEDDY. Of course I do. But I'd like to go back and see the
boys now.

Pause.

RUTH. Don't you like your family?

TEDDY. Which family?

RUTH. Your family here.

TEDDY. Of course I like them. What are you talking about?

Pause.

RUTH. You don't like them as much as you thought you did?

TEDDY. Of course I do. Of course I . . . like them. I don't
know what you're talking about.

Pause.

Listen. You know what time of the day it is there now, do
you?

RUTH. What?

TEDDY. It's morning. It's about eleven o'clock.

RUTH. Is it?

TEDDY. Yes, they're about six hours behind us . . . I mean
. . . behind the time here. The boys'll be at the pool . . .
now . . . swimming. Think of it. Morning over there. Sun.
We'll go anyway, mmnn? It's so clean there.

RUTH. Clean.

TEDDY. Yes.

RUTH. Is it dirty here?

TEDDY. No, of course not. But it's cleaner there.

Pause.

Look, I just brought you back to meet the family, didn't I? You've met them, we can go. The fall semester will be starting soon.

RUTH. You find it dirty here?

TEDDY. I didn't say I found it dirty here.

Pause.

I didn't say that.

Pause.

Look. I'll go and pack. You rest for a while. Will you? They won't be back for at least an hour. You can sleep. Rest. Please.

She looks at him.

You can help me with my lectures when we get back. I'd love that. I'd be so grateful for it, really. We can bathe till October. You know that. Here, there's nowhere to bathe, except the swimming bath down the road. You know what it's like? It's like a urinal. A filthy urinal!

Pause.

You liked Venice, didn't you? It was lovely, wasn't it? You had a good week. I mean . . . I took you there. I can speak Italian.

RUTH. But if I'd been a nurse in the Italian campaign I would have been there before.

Pause.

TEDDY. You just rest. I'll go and pack.

TEDDY *goes out and up the stairs.*

She closes her eyes.
LENNY appears from U.L.
He walks into the room and sits near her.
She opens her eyes.
Silence.

LENNY. Well, the evenings are drawing in.
RUTH. Yes, it's getting dark.

Pause.

LENNY. Winter'll soon be upon us. Time to renew one's wardrobe.

Pause.

RUTH. That's a good thing to do.
LENNY. What?

Pause.

RUTH. I always . . .

Pause.

Do you like clothes?
LENNY. Oh, yes. Very fond of clothes.

Pause.

RUTH. I'm fond . . .

Pause.

What do you think of my shoes?
LENNY. They're very nice.
RUTH. No, I can't get the ones I want over there.
LENNY. Can't get them over there, eh?
RUTH. No . . . you don't get them there.

Pause.

I was a model before I went away.

LENNY. Hats?

Pause.

I bought a girl a hat once. We saw it in a glass case, in a shop. I tell you what it had. It had a bunch of daffodils on it, tied with a black satin bow, and then it was covered with a cloche of black veiling. A cloche. I'm telling you. She was made for it.

RUTH. No ... I was a model for the body. A photographic model for the body.

LENNY. Indoor work?

RUTH. That was before I had ... all my children.

Pause.

No, not always indoors.

Pause.

Once or twice we went to a place in the country, by train. Oh, six or seven times. We used to pass a ... a large white water tower. This place ... this house ... was very big ... the trees ... there was a lake, you see ... we used to change and walk down towards the lake ... we went down a path ... on stones ... there were ... on this path. Oh, just ... wait ... yes ... when we changed in the house we had a drink. There was a cold buffet.

Pause.

Sometimes we stayed in the house but ... most often ... we walked down to the lake ... and did our modelling there.

Pause.

Just before we went to America I went down there. I walked

from the station to the gate and then I walked up the drive.
There were lights on . . . I stood in the drive . . . the
house was very light.

> TEDDY *comes down the stairs with the cases. He puts them
> down, looks at* LENNY.

TEDDY. What have you been saying to her?

> *He goes to* RUTH.

Here's your coat.

> LENNY *goes to the radiogram and puts on a record of slow
> jazz.*

Ruth. Come on. Put it on.
LENNY (*to* RUTH). What about one dance before you go?
TEDDY. We're going.
LENNY. Just one.
TEDDY. No. We're going.
LENNY. Just one dance, with her brother-in-law, before she
goes.

> LENNY *bends to her.*

Madam?

> RUTH *stands. They dance, slowly.*
> TEDDY *stands, with* RUTH'S coat.
> MAX *and* JOEY *come in the front door and into the room.
> They stand.*
> LENNY *kisses* RUTH. *They stand, kissing.*

JOEY. Christ, she's wide open.

> *Pause.*

She's a tart.

> *Pause.*

Old Lenny's got a tart in here.

> JOEY *goes to them. He takes* RUTH'S *arm. He smiles at*
> LENNY. *He sits with* RUTH *on the sofa, embraces and kisses*
> *her.*
> *He looks up at* LENNY.

Just up my street.

> *He leans her back until she lies beneath him. He kisses her.*
> *He looks up at* TEDDY *and* MAX.

It's better than a rubdown, this.

> LENNY *sits on the arm of the sofa. He caresses* RUTH'S *hair*
> *as* JOEY *embraces her.*
> MAX *comes forward, looks at the cases.*

MAX. You going. Teddy? Already?

> *Pause.*

Well, when you coming over again, eh? Look, next time you
come over, don't forget to let us know beforehand whether
you're married or not. I'll always be glad to meet the wife.
Honest. I'm telling you.

> JOEY *lies heavily on* RUTH.
> *They are almost still.*
> LENNY *caresses her hair.*

Listen, you think I don't know why you didn't tell me you
were married? I know why. You were ashamed. You thought
I'd be annoyed because you married a woman beneath you.
You should have known me better. I'm broadminded. I'm
a broadminded man.

> *He peers to see* RUTH'S *face under* JOEY, *turns back to*
> TEDDY.

Mind you, she's a lovely girl. A beautiful woman. And a

mother too. A mother of three. You've made a happy woman out of her. It's something to be proud of. I mean, we're talking about a woman of quality. We're talking about a woman of feeling.

> JOEY *and* RUTH *roll off the sofa on to the floor.*
> JOEY *clasps her.* LENNY *moves to stand above them. He looks down on them. He touches* RUTH *gently with his foot.*
> RUTH *suddenly pushes* JOEY *away.*
> *She stands up.*
> JOEY *gets to his feet, stares at her.*

RUTH. I'd like something to eat. (*To* LENNY.) I'd like a drink. Did you get any drink?

LENNY. We've got drink.

RUTH. I'd like one, please.

LENNY. What drink?

RUTH. Whisky.

LENNY. I've got it.

> *Pause.*

RUTH. Well, get it.

> LENNY *goes to the sideboard, takes out bottle and glasses.*
> JOEY *moves towards her.*

Put the record off.

> *He looks at her, turns, puts the record off.*

I want something to eat.

> *Pause.*

JOEY. I can't cook. (*Pointing to* MAX.) He's the cook.

> LENNY *brings her a glass of whisky.*

LENNY. Soda on the side?

RUTH. What's this glass? I can't drink out of this. Haven't you got a tumbler?

LENNY. Yes.

RUTH. Well, put it in a tumbler.

He takes the glass back, pours whisky into a tumbler, brings it to her.

LENNY. On the rocks? Or as it comes?

RUTH. Rocks? What do you know about rocks?

LENNY. We've got rocks. But they're frozen stiff in the fridge.

RUTH *drinks*.

LENNY *looks round at the others*.

Drinks all round?

He goes to the sideboard and pours drinks.

JOEY *moves closer to* RUTH.

OEY. What food do you want?

RUTH *walks round the room*.

RUTH (*to* TEDDY). Has your family read your critical works?

MAX. That's one thing I've never done. I've never read one of his critical works.

TEDDY. You wouldn't understand them.

LENNY *hands drinks all round*.

JOEY. What sort of food do you want? I'm not the cook, anyway.

LENNY. Soda, Ted? Or as it comes?

TEDDY. You wouldn't understand my works. You wouldn't have the faintest idea of what they were about. You wouldn't appreciate the points of reference. You're way behind. All of you. There's no point in my sending you my works. You'd be lost. It's nothing to do with the question of intelligence. It's a way of being able to look at the world. It's a question of how far you can operate on things and not in things. I mean it's a question of your capacity to ally the two, to relate the two, to balance the two. To see, to be able to *see*! I'm the one who can see. That's why I can write my critical works. Might do you good . . . have a look at them . . . see how certain people can view . . . things . . . how certain people can maintain . . . intellectual equilibrium. Intellectual equilibrium. You're just objects. You just . . . move about. I can observe it. I can see what you do. It's the same as I do. But you're lost in it. You won't get me being . . . I won't be lost in it.

BLACKOUT.
LIGHTS UP.
Evening.
TEDDY *sitting, in his coat, the cases by him.* SAM.
Pause.

SAM. Do you remember MacGregor, Teddy?
TEDDY. Mac?
SAM. Yes.
TEDDY. Of course I do.
SAM. What did you think of him? Did you take to him?
TEDDY. Yes. I liked him. Why?

Pause.

SAM. You know, you were always my favourite, of the lads. Always.

Pause.

When you wrote to me from America I was very touched, you know. I mean you'd written to your father a few times but you'd never written to me. But then, when I got that letter from you . . . well, I was very touched. I never told him. I never told him I'd heard from you.

Pause.

(*Whispering.*) Teddy, shall I tell you something? You were always your mother's favourite. She told me. It's true. You were always the . . . you were always the main object of her love.

Pause.

Why don't you stay for a couple more weeks, eh? We could have a few laughs.

LENNY *comes in the front door and into the room.*

LENNY. Still here, Ted? You'll be late for your first seminar.

He goes to the sideboard, opens it, peers in it, to the right and the left, stands.

Where's my cheese-roll?

Pause.

Someone's taken my cheese-roll. I left it there. (*To* SAM.) You been thieving?

TEDDY. I took your cheese-roll, Lenny.

Silence.
SAM *looks at them, picks up his hat and goes out of the front door.*
Silence.

LENNY. You took my cheese roll?

TEDDY. Yes.

LENNY. I made that roll myself. I cut it and put the butter on. I sliced a piece of cheese and put it in between. I put it on a plate and I put it in the sideboard. I did all that before I went out. Now I come back and you've eaten it.

TEDDY. Well, what are you going to do about it?

LENNY. I'm waiting for you to apologize.

TEDDY. But I took it deliberately, Lenny.

LENNY. You mean you didn't stumble on it by mistake?

TEDDY. No, I saw you put it there. I was hungry, so I ate it.

Pause.

LENNY. Barefaced audacity.

Pause.

What led you to be so . . . vindictive against your own brother? I'm bowled over.

Pause.

Well, Ted, I would say this is something approaching the naked truth, isn't it? It's a real cards on the table stunt. I mean, we're in the land of no holds barred now. Well, how else can you interpret it? To pinch your younger brother's specially made cheese roll when he's out doing a spot of work, that's not equivocal, it's unequivocal.

Pause.

Mind you, I will say you do seem to have grown a bit sulky during the last six years. A bit sulky. A bit inner. A bit less forthcoming. It's funny, because I'd have thought that in the United States of America, I mean with the sun and all that, the open spaces, on the old campus, in your position, lecturing, in the centre of all the intellectual life out there, on the old campus, all the social whirl, all the stimulation of it all, all your kids and all that, to have fun with, down by the pool, the Greyhound buses and all that, tons of iced water, all the comfort of those Bermuda shorts and all that, on the old campus, no time of the day or night you can't get a cup of coffee or a Dutch gin, I'd have thought you'd have grown more forthcoming, not less. Because I want you to know that you set a standard for us, Teddy. Your family looks up to you, boy, and you know what it does? It does its best to follow the example you set. Because you're a great source of pride to us. That's why we were so glad to see you come back, to welcome you back to your birthplace. That's why.

Pause.

No, listen, Ted, there's no question that we live a less rich life here than you do over there. We live a closer life. We're busy, of course. Joey's busy with his boxing, I'm busy with my occupation, Dad still plays a good game of poker, and he does the cooking as well, well up to his old standard, and Uncle Sam's the best chauffeur in the firm. But nevertheless we do make up a unit, Teddy, and you're an integral part of it. When we all sit round the backyard having a quiet gander at the night sky, there's always an empty chair standing in the circle, which is in fact yours. And so when you at length return to us, we do expect a bit of grace, a bit of je ne sais quoi, a bit of generosity of mind, a bit of liberality of spirit, to reassure us. We do expect that. But do we get it? Have we got it? Is that what you've given us?

Pause.

TEDDY. Yes.

JOEY *comes down the stairs and into the room, with a newspaper.*

LENNY (*to* JOEY). How'd you get on?
JOEY. Er . . . not bad.
LENNY. What do you mean?

Pause.

What do you mean?
JOEY. Not bad.
LENNY. I want to know what you *mean* – by not bad.
JOEY. What's it got to do with you?
LENNY. Joey, you tell your brother everything.

Pause.

JOEY. I didn't get all the way.
LENNY. You didn't get all the way?

Pause.

(*With emphasis.*) You didn't get all the way?
But you've had her up there for two hours.
JOEY. Well?
LENNY. You didn't get all the way and you've had her up there
for two hours!
JOEY. What about it?

LENNY *moves closer to him.*

LENNY. What are you telling me?
JOEY. What do you mean?
LENNY. Are you telling me she's a tease?

Pause.

She's a tease!

Pause.

What do you think of that, Ted? Your wife turns out to be
a tease. He's had her up there for two hours and he didn't
go the whole hog.
JOEY. I didn't say she was a tease.
LENNY. Are you joking? It sounds like a tease to me, don't it
to you, Ted?
TEDDY. Perhaps he hasn't got the right touch.
LENNY. Joey? Not the right touch? Don't be ridiculous. He's
had more dolly than you've had cream cakes. He's irresistible.
He's one of the few and far between. Tell him about the
last bird you had, Joey.

Pause.

JOEY. What bird?

LENNY. The last bird! When we stopped the car . . .

JOEY. Oh, that . . . yes . . . well, we were in Lenny's car one night last week . . .

LENNY. The Alfa.

JOEY. And er . . . bowling down the road . . .

LENNY. Up near the Scrubs.

JOEY. Yes, up over by the Scrubs . . .

LENNY. We were doing a little survey of North Paddington.

JOEY. And er . . . it was pretty late, wasn't it?

LENNY. Yes, it was late. Well?

Pause.

JOEY. And then we . . . well, by the kerb, we saw this parked car . . . with a couple of girls in it.

LENNY. And their escorts.

JOEY. Yes, there were two geezers in it. Anyway . . . we got out . . . and we told the . . . two escorts . . . to go away . . . which they did . . . and then we . . . got the girls out of the car . . .

LENNY. We didn't take them over the Scrubs.

JOEY. Oh, no. Not over the Scrubs. Well, the police would have noticed us there . . . you see. We took them over a bombed site.

LENNY. Rubble. In the rubble.

JOEY. Yes, plenty of rubble.

Pause.

Well . . . you know . . . then we had them.

LENNY. You've missed out the best bit. He's missed out the best bit!

JOEY. What bit?

LENNY (to TEDDY). His bird says to him, I don't mind, she says, but I've got to have some protection. I've got to have some contraceptive protection. I haven't got any contraceptive protection, old Joey says to her. In that case I won't do it, she says. Yes you will, says Joey, never mind about the contraceptive protection.

LENNY *laughs.*

Even my bird laughed when she heard that. Yes, even she gave out a bit of a laugh. So you can't say old Joey isn't a bit of a knockout when he gets going, can you? And here he is upstairs with your wife for two hours and he hasn't even been the whole hog. Well, your wife sounds like a bit of a tease to me, Ted. What do you make of it, Joey? You satisfied? Don't tell me you're satisfied without going the whole hog?

Pause.

JOEY. I've been the whole hog plenty of times. Sometimes . . . you can be happy . . . and not go the whole hog. Now and again . . . you can be happy . . . without going any hog.

LENNY *stares at him.*
MAX *and* SAM *come in the front door and into the room.*

MAX. Where's the whore? Still in bed? She'll make us all animals.
LENNY. The girl's a tease.
MAX. What?
LENNY. She's had Joey on a string.
MAX. What do you mean?
TEDDY. He had her up there for two hours and he didn't go the whole hog.

Pause.

MAX. My Joey? She did that to my boy?

Pause.

To my youngest son? Tch, tch, tch, tch. How you feeling, son? Are you all right?

JOEY. Sure I'm all right.

MAX (*to* TEDDY). Does she do that to you, too?

TEDDY. No.

LENNY. He gets the gravy.

MAX. You think so?

JOEY. No he don't.

Pause.

SAM. He's her lawful husband. She's his lawful wife.

JOEY. No he don't! He don't get no gravy! I'm telling you. I'm telling all of you. I'll kill the next man who says he gets the gravy.

MAX. Joey . . . what are you getting so excited about? (*To* LENNY.) It's because he's frustrated. You see what happens?

JOEY. Who is?

MAX. Joey. No one's saying you're wrong. In fact everyone's saying you're right.

Pause.

MAX *turns to the others.*

You know something? Perhaps it's not a bad idea to have a woman in the house. Perhaps it's a good thing. Who knows? Maybe we should keep her.

Pause.

Maybe we'll ask her if she wants to stay.

Pause.

TEDDY. I'm afraid not, Dad. She's not well, and we've got to get home to the children.

MAX. Not well? I told you, I'm used to looking after people who are not so well. Don't worry about that. Perhaps we'll keep her here.

Pause.

SAM. Don't be silly.

MAX. What's silly?

SAM. You're talking rubbish.

MAX. Me?

SAM. She's got three children.

MAX. She can have more! Here. If she's so keen.

TEDDY. She doesn't want any more.

MAX. What do you know about what she wants, eh, Ted?

TEDDY (*smiling*). The best thing for her is to come home with me, Dad. Really. We're married, you know.

   MAX *walks about the room, clicks his fingers.*

MAX. We'd have to pay her, of course. You realize that? We can't leave her walking about without any pocket money. She'll have to have a little allowance.

JOEY. Of course we'll pay her. She's got to have some money in her pocket.

MAX. That's what I'm saying. You can't expect a woman to walk about without a few bob to spend on a pair of stockings.

   Pause.

LENNY. Where's the money going to come from?

MAX. Well, how much is she worth? What we talking about, three figures?

LENNY. I asked you where the money's going to come from. It'll be an extra mouth to feed. It'll be an extra body to clothe. You realize that?

JOEY. I'll buy her clothes.

LENNY. What with?

JOEY. I'll put in a certain amount out of my wages.

MAX. That's it. We'll pass the hat round. We'll make a donation. We're all grown-up people, we've got a sense of responsibility. We'll all put a little in the hat. It's democratic.

LENNY. It'll come to a few quid, Dad.

   Pause.

I mean, she's not a woman who likes walking around in second-hand goods. She's up to the latest fashion. You wouldn't want her walking about in clothes which don't show her off at her best, would you?

MAX. Lenny, do you mind if I make a little comment? It's not meant to be critical. But I think you're concentrating too much on the economic considerations. There are other considerations. There are the human considerations. You understand what I mean? There are the human considerations. Don't forget them.

LENNY. I won't.

MAX. Well don't.

Pause.

Listen, we're bound to treat her in something approximating, at least, to the manner in which she's accustomed. After all, she's not someone off the street, she's my daughter-in-law!

JOEY. That's right.

MAX. There you are, you see. Joey'll donate, Sam'll donate.
. . .

SAM *looks at him.*

I'll put a few bob out of my pension, Lenny'll cough up. We're laughing. What about you, Ted? How much you going to put in the kitty?

TEDDY. I'm not putting anything in the kitty.

MAX. What? You won't even help to support your own wife? You lousy stinkpig. Your mother would drop dead if she heard you take that attitude.

LENNY. Eh, Dad.

LENNY *walks forward.*

I've got a better idea.

MAX. What?

LENNY. There's no need for us to go to all this expense. I know these women. Once they get started they ruin your budget. I've got a better idea. Why don't I take her up with me to Greek Street?

Pause.

MAX. You mean put her on the game?

Pause.

We'll put her on the game. That's a stroke of genius, that's a marvellous idea. You mean she can earn the money herself – on her back?

LENNY. Yes.

MAX. Wonderful. The only thing is, it'll have to be short hours. We don't want her out of the house all night.

LENNY. I can limit the hours.

MAX. How many?

LENNY. Four hours a night.

MAX (*dubiously*). Is that enough?

LENNY. She'll bring in a good sum for four hours a night.

MAX. Well, you should know. After all, it's true, the last thing we want to do is wear the girl out. She's going to have her obligations this end as well. Where you going to put her in Greek Street?

LENNY. It doesn't have to be right in Greek Street, Dad. I've got a number of flats all around that area.

MAX. You have? Well, what about me? Why don't you give me one?

LENNY. You're sexless.

JOEY. Eh, wait a minute, what's all this?

MAX. I know what Lenny's saying. Lenny's saying she can pay her own way. What do you think, Teddy? That'll solve all our problems.

JOEY. Eh, wait a minute. I don't want to share her.

MAX. What did you say?

JOEY. I don't want to share her with a lot of yobs!

MAX. Yobs! You arrogant git! What arrogance. (*To* LENNY.) Will you be supplying her with yobs?

LENNY. I've got a very distinguished clientele, Joey. They're more distinguished than you'll ever be.

MAX. So you can count yourself lucky we're including you in.

JOEY. I didn't think I was going to have to share her!

MAX. Well, you *are* going to have to share her! Otherwise she goes straight back to America. You understand?

   Pause.

It's tricky enough as it is, without you shoving your oar in. But there's something worrying me. Perhaps she's not so up to the mark. Eh? Teddy, you're the best judge. Do you think she'd be up to the mark?

   Pause.

I mean what about all this teasing? Is she going to make a habit of it? That'll get us nowhere.

   Pause.

TEDDY. It was just love play . . . I suppose . . . that's all I suppose it was.

MAX. Love play? Two bleeding hours? That's a bloody long time for love play!

LENNY. I don't think we've got anything to worry about on that score, Dad.

MAX. How do you know?

LENNY. I'm giving you a professional opinion.

   LENNY *goes to* TEDDY.

LENNY. Listen, Teddy, you could help us, actually. If I were to send you some cards, over to America . . . you know, very nice ones, with a name on, and a telephone number, very discreet, well, you could distribute them . . . to various parties, who might be making a trip over here. Of course, you'd get a little percentage out of it.

MAX. I mean, you needn't tell them she's your wife.

LENNY. No, we'd call her something else. Dolores, or something.

MAX. Or Spanish Jacky.

LENNY. No, you've got to be reserved about it, Dad. We could call her something nice . . . like Cynthia . . . or Gillian.

Pause.

JOEY. Gillian.

Pause.

LENNY. No, what I mean, Teddy, you must know lots of professors, heads of departments, men like that. They pop over here for a week at the Savoy, they need somewhere they can go to have a nice quiet poke. And of course you'd be in a position to give them inside information.

MAX. Sure. You can give them proper data. I bet you before two months we'd have a waiting list.

LENNY. You could be our representative in the States.

MAX. Of course. We're talking in international terms! By the time we've finished Pan-American'll give us a discount.

Pause.

TEDDY. She'd get old . . . very quickly.

MAX. No . . . not in this day and age! With the health service? Old! How could she get old? She'll have the time of her life.

RUTH *comes down the stairs, dressed.*
She comes into the room.
She smiles at the gathering, and sits.
Silence.

TEDDY. Ruth . . . the family have invited you to stay, for a little while longer. As a . . . as a kind of guest. If you like the idea I don't mind. We can manage very easily at home . . . until you come back.

RUTH. How very nice of them.

Pause.

MAX. It's an offer from our heart.

RUTH. It's very sweet of you.

MAX. Listen . . . it would be our pleasure.

Pause.

RUTH. I think I'd be too much trouble.

MAX. Trouble? What are you talking about? What trouble? Listen, I'll tell you something. Since poor Jessie died, eh, Sam? we haven't had a woman in the house. Not one. Inside this house. And I'll tell you why. Because their mother's image was so dear any other woman would have . . . tarnished it. But you . . . Ruth . . . you're not only lovely and beautiful, but you're kin. You're kith. You belong here.

Pause.

RUTH. I'm very touched.

MAX. Of course you're touched. I'm touched.

Pause.

TEDDY. But Ruth, I should tell you . . . that you'll have to pull your weight a little, if you stay. Financially. My father isn't very well off.

RUTH (*to* MAX). Oh, I'm sorry.

MAX. No, you'd just have to bring in a little, that's all. A few pennies. Nothing much. It's just that we're waiting for Joey to hit the top as a boxer. When Joey hits the top . . . well . . .

Pause.

TEDDY. Or you can come home with me.
LENNY. We'd get you a flat.

Pause.

RUTH. A flat?
LENNY. Yes.
RUTH. Where?
LENNY. In town.

Pause.

But you'd live here, with us.
MAX. Of course you would. This would be your home. In the bosom of the family.
LENNY. You'd just pop up to the flat a couple of hours a night, that's all.
MAX. Just a couple of hours, that's all. That's all.
LENNY. And you make enough money to keep you going here.

Pause.

RUTH. How many rooms would this flat have?
LENNY. Not many.
RUTH. I would want at least three rooms and a bathroom.
LENNY. You wouldn't need three rooms and a bathroom.
MAX. She'd need a bathroom.
LENNY. But not three rooms.

Pause.

RUTH. Oh, I would. Really.
LENNY. Two would do.
RUTH. No. Two wouldn't be enough.

Pause.

I'd want a dressing-room, a rest-room, and a bedroom.

Pause.

LENNY. All right, we'll get you a flat with three rooms and a bathroom.

RUTH. With what kind of conveniences?

LENNY. All conveniences.

RUTH. A personal maid?

LENNY. Of course.

Pause.

We'd finance you, to begin with, and then, when you were established, you could pay us back, in instalments.

RUTH. Oh, no, I wouldn't agree to that.

LENNY. Oh, why not?

RUTH. You would have to regard your original outlay simply as a capital investment.

Pause.

LENNY. I see. All right.

RUTH. You'd supply my wardrobe, of course?

LENNY. We'd supply everything. Everything you need.

RUTH. I'd need an awful lot. Otherwise I wouldn't be content.

LENNY. You'd have everything.

RUTH. I would naturally want to draw up an inventory of everything I would need, which would require your signatures in the presence of witnesses.

LENNY. Naturally.

RUTH. All aspects of the agreement and conditions of employment would have to be clarified to our mutual satisfaction before we finalized the contract.

LENNY. Of course.

Pause.

RUTH. Well, it might prove a workable arrangement.

LENNY. I think so.

MAX. And you'd have the whole of your daytime free, of course. You could do a bit of cooking here if you wanted to.

LENNY. Make the beds.

MAX. Scrub the place out a bit.

TEDDY. Keep everyone company.

SAM comes forward.

SAM (*in one breath*). MacGregor had Jessie in the back of my cab as I drove them along.

He croaks and collapses.
He lies still.
They look at him.

MAX. What's he done? Dropped dead?

LENNY. Yes.

MAX. A corpse? A corpse on my floor? Get him out of here! Clear him out of here!

JOEY bends over SAM.

JOEY. He's not dead.

LENNY. He probably was dead, for about thirty seconds.

MAX. He's not even dead!

LENNY looks down at SAM.

LENNY. Yes, there's still some breath there.

MAX (*pointing at SAM*). You know what that man had?

LENNY. Has.

MAX. Has! A diseased imagination.

Pause.

RUTH. Yes, it sounds a very attractive idea.

MAX. Do you want to shake on it now, or do you want to leave it till later?

RUTH. Oh, we'll leave it till later.

TEDDY stands.
He looks down at SAM.

TEDDY. I was going to ask him to drive me to London Airport.

He goes to the cases, picks one up.

Well, I'll leave your case, Ruth. I'll just go up the road to the Underground.

MAX. Listen, if you go the other way, first left, first right, you remember, you might find a cab passing there.

TEDDY. Yes, I might do that.

MAX. Or you can take the tube to Piccadilly Circus, won't take you ten minutes, and pick up a cab from there out to the Airport.

TEDDY. Yes, I'll probably do that.

MAX. Mind you, they'll charge you double fare. They'll charge you for the return trip. It's over the six-mile limit.

TEDDY. Yes. Well, bye-bye, Dad. Look after yourself.

They shake hands.

MAX. Thanks, son. Listen. I want to tell you something. It's been wonderful to see you.

Pause.

TEDDY. It's been wonderful to see you.

MAX. Do your boys know about me? Eh? Would they like to see a photo, do you think, of their grandfather?

TEDDY. I know they would.

MAX *brings out his wallet.*

MAX. I've got one on me. I've got one here. Just a minute. Here you are. Will they like that one?

TEDDY (*taking it*). They'll be thrilled.

He turns to LENNY.

Good-bye, Lenny.

They shake hands.

LENNY. Ta-ta, Ted. Good to see you. Have a good trip.

TEDDY. Bye-bye, Joey.

> JOEY *does not move.*

JOEY. Ta-ta.

> TEDDY *goes to the front door.*

RUTH. Eddie.

> TEDDY *turns.*
> *Pause.*

Don't become a stranger.

> TEDDY *goes, shuts the front door.*
> *Silence.*
> *The three men stand.*
> RUTH *sits relaxed on her chair.*
> SAM *lies still.*
> JOEY *walks slowly across the room.*
> *He kneels at her chair.*
> *She touches his head, lightly.*
> *He puts his head in her lap.*
> MAX *begins to move above them, backwards and forwards.*
> LENNY *stands still.*
> MAX *turns to* LENNY.

MAX. I'm too old, I suppose. She thinks I'm an old man.

> *Pause.*

I'm not such an old man.

> *Pause.*

(*To* RUTH.) You think I'm too old for you?

> *Pause.*

Listen. You think you're just going to get that big slag all

the time? You think you're just going to have him . . .
you're going to just have him all the time? You're going to
have to work! You'll have to take them on, you understand?

Pause.

Does she realize that?

Pause.

Lenny, do you think she understands . . .

He begins to stammer.

What . . . what . . . what . . . we're getting at? What
. . . we've got in mind? Do you think she's got it clear?

Pause.

I don't think she's got it clear.

Pause.

You understand what I mean? Listen, I've got a funny idea
she'll do the dirty on us, you want to bet? She'll use us,
she'll make use of us, I can tell you! I can smell it! You
want to bet?

Pause.

She won't . . . be adaptable!

*He begins to groan, clutches his stick, falls on to his knees by the
side of her chair. His body sags. The groaning stops. His body
straightens. He looks at her, still kneeling.*

I'm not an old man.

Pause.

Do you hear me?

He raises his face to her.

Kiss me.

She continues to touch JOEY'S *head, lightly.*
LENNY *stands, watching.*

Curtain

TEA PARTY

Tea Party was commissioned by sixteen member countries of the European Broadcasting Union, to be transmitted by all of them under the title, *The Largest Theatre in the World*. It was first presented by B.B.C. Television on 25 March 1965 with the following cast:

DISSON	Leo McKern
WENDY	Vivien Merchant
DIANA	Jennifer Wright
WILLY	Charles Gray
DISLEY	John Le Mesurier
LOIS	Margaret Denyer
FATHER	Frederick Piper
MOTHER	Hilda Barry
TOM	Peter Bartlett
JOHN	Robert Bartlett

Directed by Charles Jarrott

Tea Party and *The Basement* opened at the Duchess Theatre on 17 September 1970, directed by James Hammerstein and produced by Eddie Kulukundis for Knightsbridge Theatrical Productions Ltd., with the following cast:

TEA PARTY

DISSON	Donald Pleasence
WENDY	Vivien Merchant
DIANA	Gabrielle Drake
WILLY	Barry Foster
TOM	Robin Angell
JOHN	Kevin Chippendale
DISLEY	Derek Aylward
LOIS	Jill Johnson
FATHER	Arthur Hewlett
MOTHER	Hilda Barry

THE BASEMENT

LAW	Donald Pleasence
STOTT	Barry Foster
JANE	Stephanie Beacham

TEA PARTY

An electric lift rising to the top floor of an office block. WENDY
stands in it.

Corridor.
*The lift comes to rest in a broad carpeted corridor, the interior of
an office suite. It is well appointed, silent. The walls are papered
with Japanese silk. Along the walls in alcoves are set, at various
intervals, a selection of individually designed wash basins, water
closets and bidets, all lit by hooded spotlights.*
WENDY *steps out of the lift and walks down the corridor towards
a door. She knocks. It opens.*

Disson's office. Morning.
DISSON *rising from a large desk. He goes round the desk to meet*
WENDY *and shakes her hand.*
DISSON. How do you do, Miss Dodd? Nice of you to come.
  Please sit down.
    DISSON *goes back to his seat behind the desk.* WENDY *sits
    in a chair at the corner of the desk.*
  That's right.
    He refers to papers on the desk.
  Well now, I've had a look at your references. They seem to
  be excellent. You've had quite a bit of experience.
WENDY. Yes, sir.
DISSON. Not in my line, of course. We manufacture sanitary
  ware . . . but I suppose you know that?
WENDY. Yes, of course I do, Mr Disson.
DISSON. You've heard of us, have you?
WENDY. Oh yes.
    WENDY *crosses her left leg over her right.*

DISSON. Well, do you think you'd be interested in . . . in this area of work?

WENDY. Oh, certainly, sir, yes, I think I would.

DISSON. We're the most advanced sanitary engineers in the country. I think I can say that quite confidently.

WENDY. Yes, I believe so.

DISSON. Oh yes. We manufacture more bidets than anyone else in England. (*He laughs.*) It's almost by way of being a mission. Cantilever units, hidden cisterns, footpedals, you know, things like that.

WENDY. Footpedals?

DISSON. Instead of a chain or plug. A footpedal.

WENDY. Oh. How marvellous.

DISSON. They're growing more popular every day and rightly so.

WENDY *crosses her right leg over her left.*

Well now, this . . . post is, in fact, that of my personal assistant. Did you understand that? A very private secretary, in fact. And a good deal of responsibility would undoubtedly devolve upon you. Would you . . . feel yourself capable of discharging it?

WENDY. Once I'd correlated all the fundamental features of the work, sir, I think so, yes.

DISSON. All the fundamental features, yes. Good.

WENDY *crosses her left leg over her right.*

I see you left your last job quite suddenly.

Pause.

May I ask the reason?

WENDY. Well, it's . . . a little embarrassing, sir.

DISSON. Really?

Pause.

Well, I think I should know, don't you? Come on, you can tell me. What was it?

WENDY *straightens her skirt over her knees.*

WENDY. Well, it is rather personal, Mr Disson.

DISSON. Yes, but I think I should know, don't you?

Pause.

WENDY.Well, it's simply that I couldn't persuade my chief . . . to call a halt to his attentions.

DISSON. *What?* (*He consults the papers on the desk.*) A firm of this repute? It's unbelievable.

WENDY. I'm afraid it's true, sir.

Pause.

DISSON. What sort of attentions?

WENDY. Oh, I don't . . .

DISSON.What sort?

Pause.

WENDY. He never stopped touching me, Mr Disson, that's all.

DISSON. Touching you?

WENDY. Yes.

DISSON. Where? (*Quickly.*) That must have been very disturbing for you.

WENDY. Well, quite frankly, it is disturbing, to be touched all the time.

DISSON. Do you mean at every opportunity?

WENDY. Yes, sir.

Slight pause.

DISSON. Did you cry?

WENDY. Cry?

DISSON. Did he make you cry?

WENDY. Oh just a little, occasionally, sir.

DISSON. What a monster.

Slight pause.

Well, I do sympathize.

WENDY. Thank you, sir.

DISSON. One would have thought this . . . tampering, this . . . interfering . . . with secretaries was something of the past, a myth, in fact, something that only took place in paperback books. Tch. Tch.

WENDY *crosses her right leg over her left.*

Anyway, be that as it may, your credentials are excellent
and I would say you possessed an active and inquiring
intelligence and a pleasing demeanour, two attributes I consider necessary for this post. I'd like you to start immediately.

WENDY. Oh, that's wonderful. Thank you so much, Mr Disson.

DISSON. Not at all.

> *They stand. He walks across the room to another desk.*

This'll be your desk.

WENDY. Ah.

DISSON. There are certain personal arrangements I'd like you
to check after lunch. I'm . . . getting married tomorrow.

WENDY. Oh, congratulations.

DISSON. Thanks. Yes, this is quite a good week for me, what
with one thing and another.

> *The telephone rings on his desk.*
>
> *He crosses and picks it up.*

Hullo, Disley. How are you? . . . What? Oh my goodness,
don't say that.

Disson's house. Sitting-room. Evening.

DIANA. This is my brother Willy.

DISSON. I'm very glad to meet you.

WILLY. And I you. Congratulations.

DISSON. Thank you.

DIANA (*giving him a drink*). Here you are, Robert.

DISSON. Thanks. Cheers.

DIANA. Cheers.

WILLY. To tomorrow.

DISSON. Yes.

> *They drink.*

I'm afraid we've run into a bit of trouble.

DIANA. Why?

DISSON. I've lost my best man.

DIANA. Oh no.

DISSON (*to* WILLY). My oldest friend. Man called Disley. Gastric flu. Can't make it tomorrow.

WILLY. Oh dear.

DISSON. He was going to make a speech at the reception – in my honour. A superb speech. I read it. Now he can't make it.

Pause.

WILLY. Isn't there anyone else you know?

DISSON. Yes, of course. But not like him . . . you see. I mean, he was the natural choice.

DIANA. How infuriating.

Pause.

WILLY. Well, look, I can be your best man, if you like.

DIANA. How can you, Willy? You're giving me away.

WILLY. Oh yes.

DISSON. Oh, the best man's not important; you can always get a best man – all he's got to do is stand there; it's the speech that's important, the speech in honour of the groom. Who's going to make the speech?

Pause.

WILLY. Well, I can make the speech, if you like.

DISSON. But how can you make a speech in honour of the groom when you're making one in honour of the bride?

WILLY. Does that matter?

DIANA. No. Why does it?

DISSON. Yes, but look . . . I mean, thanks very much . . . but the fact is . . . that you don't know me, do you? I mean we've only just met. Disley knows me well, that's the thing, you see. His speech centred around our long-standing friendship. I mean, what he knew of my character . . .

WILLY. Yes, of course, of course. No, look, all I'm saying is that I'm willing to have a crack at it if there's no other solution. Willing to come to the aid of the party, as it were.

DIANA. He *is* a wonderful speaker, Robert.

Wedding reception. Private room. Exclusive restaurant.

DISSON, DIANA, WILLY, DISSON'S PARENTS, DISSON'S
SONS. WILLY *is speaking.*

WILLY. I remember the days my sister and I used to swim
together in the lake at Sunderley. The grace of her crawl,
even then, as a young girl. I can remember those long
summer evenings at Sunderley, my mother and I crossing
the lawn towards the terrace and through the great windows
hearing my sister play Brahms. The delicacy of her touch.
My mother and I would, upon entering the music room,
gaze in silence at Diana's long fingers moving in exquisite
motion on the keys. As for our father, our father knew no
pleasure keener than watching his daughter at her needle-
work. A man whose business was the State's, a man eternally
active, his one great solace from the busy world would be to
sit for hours on end at a time watching his beloved daughter
ply her needle. Diana – my sister – was the dear grace of
our household, the flower, the blossom, and the bloom. One
can only say to the groom: Groom, your fortune is im-
measurable.

  Applause. DIANA *kisses him.*
  DISSON *shakes his hand warmly.*

TOASTMASTER. My lords, reverend gentlemen, ladies and
gentlemen, pray silence for Mr William Pierrepoint Torrance, who will propose the toast in honour of the groom.
  WILLY *turns. Applause.*

WILLY. I have not known Robert for a long time, in fact I have
known him only for a very short time. But in that short time
I have found him to be a man of integrity, honesty and
humility. After a modest beginning, he has built his business
up into one of the proudest and most vigorous in the land.
And this – almost alone. Now he has married a girl who
equals, if not surpasses, his own austere standards of
integrity. He has married my sister, who possesses within
her that rare and uncommon attribute known as inner beauty,

not to mention the loveliness of her exterior. Par excellence
as a woman with a needle, beyond excellence as a woman of
taste, discernment, sensibility and imagination. An excellent
swimmer who, in all probability, has the beating of her
husband in the two hundred metres breast stroke.

Laughter and applause.

WILLY *waits for silence.*

It is to our parents that she owes her candour, her elegance
of mind, her *sensibilité*. Our parents, who, though gone, have
not passed from us, but who are here now on this majestic
day, and offer you their welcome, the bride their love, and
the groom their congratulations.

Applause. DIANA *kisses him.*

DISSON *shakes his hand warmly.*

DISSON. Marvellous.

WILLY. Diana, I want to tell you something.

DIANA. What?

WILLY. You have married a good man. He will make you
happy.

DIANA. I know.

DISSON. Wonderful speeches. Wonderful. Listen. What are
you doing these days?

WILLY. Nothing much.

TOASTMASTER. My lords . . .

DISSON (*whispering*). How would you like to come in with me
for a bit? See how you like it, how you get on. Be my second
in command. Office of your own. Plenty of room for initiative.

TOASTMASTER. My lords, reverend gentlemen, ladies and
gentlemen –

WILLY. Marvellous idea. I'll say yes at once.

DISSON. Good.

DIANA *kisses* DISSON.

DIANA. Darling.

TOASTMASTER. Pray silence for the groom.

DISSON *moves forward.*

Applause. Silence.

DISSON. This is the happiest day of my life.

Sumptuous hotel room. Italy.
The light is on. The camera rests at the foot of the bed. The characters are not seen. Their voices heard only.

DISSON. Are you happy?

DIANA. Yes.

DISSON. Very happy?

DIANA. Yes.

DISSON. Have you ever been happier? With any other man?

DIANA. Never.

Pause.

DISSON. I make you happy, don't I? Happier than you've ever been . . . with any other man.

DIANA. Yes. You do.

Pause.

Yes.

Silence.

Disson's house. Workroom.

DISSON *at his workbench. With sandpaper and file he is putting the finishing touches to a home-made model yacht. He completes the job, dusts the yacht, sets it on a shelf and looks at it with satisfaction.*

Disson's house. Breakfast room. Morning.

DISSON *and* DIANA *at the table.*

DISSON. Your eyes are shining.

Pause.

They're shining.

DIANA. Mmmnnn.

DISSON. They've been shining for months.

DIANA (*smiling*). My eyes? Have they?

DISSON. Every morning.

Pause.

I'm glad you didn't marry that . . . Jerry . . . whatever-hisnamewas . . .

DIANA. Oh, him . . .

DISSON. Why didn't you?

DIANA. He was weak.

Pause.

DISSON. I'm not weak.

DIANA. No.

DISSON. Am I?

He takes her hand.

DIANA. You're strong.

THE TWINS enter the room.

THE TWINS mutter, 'Morning'.

DIANA and DISSON say 'Good Morning'.

Silence. THE TWINS sit. DIANA pours tea for them. They butter toast, take marmalade, begin to eat.

Silence.

Would you like eggs?

TOM. No, thanks.

DIANA. John?

Silence.

DISSON. John!

JOHN. What?

DISSON. Don't say what!

JOHN. What shall I say?

DIANA. Would you like eggs?

Pause.

JOHN. Oh.

Pause.

No, thanks.

The boys giggle and eat. Silence.

JOHN *whispers to* TOM.

DISSON. What are you saying? Speak up.

JOHN. Nothing.

DISSON. Do you think I'm deaf?

TOM. I've never thought about it.

DISSON. I wasn't talking to you. I was talking to John.

JOHN. Me? Sorry, sir.

DISSON. Now don't be silly. You've never called me sir before. That's rather a daft way to address your father.

JOHN. Uncle Willy called his father sir. He told me.

DISSON. Yes, but you don't call *me* sir! Do you understand?

Willy's office. Morning.

DISSON *leads* WILLY *in.*

DISSON. Here you are, Willy. This'll be your office. How'd you like it?

WILLY. First rate.

DISSON. These two offices are completely cut off from the rest of the staff. They're all on the lower floor. Our only contact is by intercom, unless I need to see someone personally, which is rare. Equally, I dislike fraternization between the two offices. We shall meet only by strict arrangement, otherwise we'll never get any work done. That suit you?

WILLY. Perfectly.

DISSON. There was a man in here, but I got rid of him.

DISSON *leads* WILLY *through a communicating door into his own office.*

Disson's office.

On a side table coffee is set for two.

DISSON *goes to the table and pours.*

DISSON. I think I should explain to you the sort of man I am.

I'm a thorough man. I like things to be done and done well.
I don't like dithering. I don't like indulgence. I don't like
self-doubt. I don't like fuzziness. I like clarity. Clear inten-
tion. Precise execution. Black or white?

WILLY. White, please.

DISSON. But I've no patience with conceit and self-regard. A
man's job is to assess his powers coolly and correctly and
equally the powers of others. Having done this, he can pro-
ceed to establish a balanced and reasonable relationship with
his fellows. In my view, living is a matter of active and willing
participation. So is work. Sugar?

WILLY. Two, please.

DISSON. Now, dependence isn't a word I would use lightly,
but I will use it and I don't regard it as a weakness. To understand the meaning of the term dependence is to understand
that one's powers are limited and that to live with others is
not only sensible but the only way work can be done and
dignity achieved. Nothing is more sterile or lamentable than
the man content to live within himself. I've always made it
my business to be on the most direct possible terms with the
members of my staff and the body of my business associates.
And by my example opinions are declared freely, without
shame or deception. It seems to me essential that we cultivate
the ability to operate lucidly upon our problems and therefore be in a position to solve them. That's why your sister
loves me. I don't play about at the periphery of matters. I
go right to the centre. I believe life can be conducted
efficiently. I never waste my energies in any kind of timorous
expectation. Neither do I ask to be loved. I expect to be
given only what I've worked for. If you make a plum pudding,
what do you do with it? You don't shove it up on a shelf.
You stick a knife into it and eat it. Everything has a function.
In other words, if we're to work together we must appreciate
that interdependence is the key word, that it's your job to
understand me and mine to understand you. Agreed?

WILLY. Absolutely.

DISSON. Now, the first thing you need is a secretary. We'll get on to it at once.

WILLY. Can I suggest someone? I know she's very keen and, I'd say, very competent.

DISSON. Who?

WILLY. My sister.

   Pause.

DISSON. Your sister? You mean my wife?

WILLY. She told me she'd love to do it.

DISSON. She hasn't told me.

WILLY. She's shy.

DISSON. But she doesn't need to work. Why should she want to work?

WILLY. To be closer to you.

Willy's office.

WILLY *and* DIANA *at their desks, both examining folders intently.*
   Silence.

Disson's office.

DISSON *and* WENDY *at their desks.* WENDY *typing on an electric typewriter.* DISSON *looking out of the window.* DISSON *turns from the window, glances at the door leading to* WILLY'S *office. The intercom buzzes on* WENDY'S *desk. She switches through.*

WENDY. Mr Disson does not want to be disturbed until 3.30.

   DISSON *glances again at* WILLY'S *door.*
   Silence.

Disson's house. Sitting-room. Early evening.

DIANA *and* THE TWINS *are sitting about, reading.*

DIANA. Do you miss your mother?

JOHN. We didn't know her very well. We were very young when she died.

DIANA. Your father has looked after you and brought you up very well.

JOHN. Oh, thank you. He'll be pleased to hear that.

DIANA. I've told him.

JOHN. What did he say?

DIANA. He was pleased I thought so. You mean a great deal to him.

JOHN. Children seem to mean a great deal to their parents, I've noticed. Though I've often wondered what 'a great deal' means.

TOM. I've often wondered what 'mean' means.

DIANA. Aren't you proud of your father's achievements?

JOHN. We are. I should say we are.

Pause.

DIANA. And now that your father has married again . . . has the change in your life affected you very much?

JOHN. What change?

DIANA. Living with me.

JOHN. Ah. Well, I think there definitely is an adjustment to be made. Wouldn't you say that, Tom?

DIANA. Of course there is. But would you say it's an easy adjustment to make, or difficult?

JOHN. Well, it really all depends on how good you are at making adjustments. We're very good at making adjustments, aren't we, Tom?

The front door slams. DIANA *and* THE TWINS *look down at their books.* DISSON *comes in. They all look up, smile.*

DISSON. Hullo.

They all smile genially at him.

DISSON *looks quickly from one to the other.*

Disson's office. Morning.
Sun shining in the window. DISSON *at his desk.* WENDY *at the*
cabinet. He watches her. She turns.

WENDY. Isn't it a beautiful day, Mr Disson?

DISSON. Close the curtains.

> WENDY *closes the curtains.*

Got your pad?

WENDY. Yes, sir.

DISSON. Sit down.

> WENDY *sits in a chair by the corner of his desk.*

Warwick and Sons. We duly acknowledge receipt of your
letter of the twenty-first inst. There should be no difficulty
in meeting your requirements. What's the matter?

WENDY. Sir?

DISSON. You're wriggling.

WENDY. I'm sorry, sir.

DISSON. Is it the chair?

WENDY. Mmn . . . it might be.

DISSON. Too hard, I expect. A little hard for you.

> *Pause.*

Is that it?

WENDY. A little.

DISSON. Sit on the desk.

WENDY. The desk?

DISSON. Yes, on the leather.

> *Slight pause.*

It'll be softer . . . for you.

WENDY. Well, that'll be nice.

> *Pause.* WENDY *eventually uncrosses her legs and stands. She*
> *looks at the desk.*

I think it's a little high . . . to get up on.

DISSON. Of course it isn't.

WENDY (*looking at the desk*). Hmmmn-mmmn . . .

DISSON. Go on, get up. You couldn't call that high.

WENDY *places her back to the desk and slowly attempts to raise herself up on to it.*

She stops.

WENDY. I think I'll have to put my feet on the chair, really, to hoist myself up.

DISSON. You can hoist yourself up without using your feet.

WENDY (*dubiously*). Well . . .

DISSON. Look, get up or stay down. Make up your mind. One thing or the other. I want to get on with my letter to Birmingham.

WENDY. I was just wondering if you'd mind if I put my high-heeled shoes on your chair . . . to help me get up.

Pause.

DISSON. I don't mind.

WENDY. But I'm worried in case my heels might chip the wood. They're rather sharp, these heels.

DISSON. Are they?

Pause.

Well, try it, anyway. You won't chip the wood.

WENDY *puts her feet on the chair and hoists herself up on to the desk.*

He watches.

WENDY *settles herself on the desk and picks up her pen and pad. She reads from the pad.*

WENDY. There should be no difficulty in meeting your requirements.

Disson's house. Games room. Day.

DISSON *and* WILLY *are playing ping-pong.* THE TWINS *watch.*

A long rally. DISSON *backhand flips to win the point.*

JOHN. Good shot, Dad.

TOM. Thirteen-eighteen.

WILLY. Your backhand's in form, Robert.

JOHN. Attack his forehand.

WILLY *serves. A rally.* WILLY *attacks* DISSON'S *forehand.*
DISSON *moves over to his right and then flips backhand to*
win the point. THE TWINS *applaud.*

TOM. Thirteen-nineteen.

WILLY. Backhand flip on the forehand, eh?

    WILLY *serves.*

    From DISSON'S *point of view see two balls bounce and leap*
    past both ears.

TWINS. Shot!

TOM. Fourteen-nineteen.

    DISSON *puts down his bat and walks slowly to* WILLY.

DISSON. You served two balls, old chap.

WILLY. Two balls?

DISSON. You sent me two balls.

WILLY. No, no. Only one.

DISSON. Two.

    Pause.

JOHN. One, Dad.

DISSON. What?

TOM. One.

    Pause.

    WILLY *walks to* DISSON'S *end, bends.*

WILLY. Look.

    WILLY *picks up one ball.*

  One ball. Catch!

    He throws the ball. DISSON *gropes, loses sight of the ball.*
    It bounces under the table. He crouches, leans under the table
    for it. Gets it, withdraws, looks up. WILLY *and* THE TWINS
    look down at him.

Disley's surgery.
Room darkened.
A torch shining in DISSON'S *eyes. First the left eye, then the right*
eye. Torch out. Light on.

DISLEY. There's nothing wrong with your eyes, old boy.

DISSON. Nothing?

DISLEY. They're in first-rate condition. Truly.

DISSON. That's funny.

DISLEY. I'd go as far as to say your sight was perfect.

DISSON. Huh.

DISLEY. Check the bottom line.

    DISLEY *switches off the light, puts on the light on the letter board.*

  What is it?

DISSON. EXJLNVCGTY.

DISLEY. Perfect.

    Board light off. Room light on.

DISSON. Yes, I know . . . I know that . . .

DISLEY. Well, what are you worried about?

DISSON. It's not that . . .

DISLEY. Colour? Do you confuse colours? Look at me. What colour am I?

DISSON. Colourless.

DISLEY (*laughs, stops*). Very funny. What distinguishing marks can you see about me?

DISSON. Two.

DISLEY. What?

DISSON. You have one grey strip in your hair, quite faint.

DISLEY. Good. What's the other?

DISSON. You have a brown stain on your left cheek.

DISLEY. A brown stain? Can you see that? (*He looks in the mirror.*) I didn't know it was so evident.

DISSON. Of course it's evident. It stains your face.

DISLEY. Don't . . . go on about it, old boy. I didn't realize it was so evident. No one's ever noticed it before.

DISSON. Not even your wife?

DISLEY. Yes, she has. Anyway, I'd say your eyes are sharp enough. What colour are those lampshades?

DISSON. They're dark blue drums. Each has a golden rim. The carpet is Indian.

DISLEY. That's not a colour.

DISSON. It's white. Over there, by that cabinet, I can see a deep black burn.

DISLEY. A burn? Where? Do you mean that shadow?

DISSON. That's not a shadow. It's a burn.

DISLEY (*looking*). So it is. How the hell did that happen?

DISSON. Listen . . . I never said I couldn't see. You don't understand. Most of the time . . . my eyesight is excellent. It always has been. But . . . it's become unreliable. It's become . . . erratic. Sometimes, quite suddenly, very occasionally, something happens . . . something . . . goes wrong . . . with my eyes.

Pause.

DISLEY. I can find no evidence that your sight is in any way deficient.

DISSON. You don't understand.

A knock at the door. LOIS *appears.*

LOIS. I'm just going out. Wanted to say hullo to you before I go.

DISSON. Hullo, Lois.

He kisses her cheek.

LOIS. You've been in here for ages. Don't tell me you need glasses?

DISLEY. His eyes are perfect.

LOIS. They look it.

DISSON. What a lovely dress you're wearing.

LOIS. Do you like it? Really?

DISSON. Of course I like it.

LOIS. You must see if the birds are still there.

She lifts the blind.

Yes, they are. They're all at the bird bath.

They all look into the garden.

Look at them. They're so happy. They love my bath. They do, really. They love it. They make me so happy, my birds. And they seem to know, instinctively, that I adore them. They do, really.

Disson's house. Bedroom. Night.

DISSON *alone, in front of a mirror.*

He is tying his tie. He ties it. The front end hangs only half-way down his chest.

He unties it, ties it again. The front end, this time, is even shorter.

He unties it, holds the tie and looks at it.

He then ties the tie again. This time the two ends are of equal length.

He breathes deeply, relaxes, goes out of the room.

Disson's house. Dining room. Night.

DIANA, WILLY, DISSON *at dinner.*

DIANA. I'd say she was a real find.

WILLY. Oh, she's of inestimable value to the firm, wouldn't you say, Robert?

DISSON. Oh yes.

DIANA. I mean for someone who's not . . . actually . . . part of us . . . I mean, an outsider . . . to give such devotion and willingness to the job, as she does . . . well, it's remarkable. We were very lucky to find her.

DISSON. I found her, actually.

WILLY. You found me, too, old boy.

DIANA (*laughing*). And me.

    Pause.

She's of course so completely trustworthy, and so very persuasive, on the telephone. I've heard her . . . when the door's been open . . . once or twice.

WILLY. Oh, splendid girl, all round.

DISSON. She's not so bloody marvellous.

    Pause. They look at him.

She's all right, she's all right. But she's not so bloody marvellous.

DIANA. Well, perhaps not quite as accomplished as I am, no.
    Do you think I'm a good private secretary, Willy?

WILLY. First rate.

    Pause. They eat and drink.

DISSON. I don't think it's a good idea for you to work.

DIANA. Me? Why not? I love it.

DISSON. I never see you. If you were at home I could take the
    occasional afternoon off . . . to see you. As it is I never
    see you. In day-time.

DIANA. You mean I'm so near and yet so far?

    Pause.

DISSON. Yes.

DIANA. Would you prefer me to be your secretary?

DISSON. No, no, of course not. That wouldn't work at all.

    Pause.

WILLY. But we do all meet at lunch-time. We meet in the
    evening.

    DISSON *looks at him.*

DIANA. But I like working. You wouldn't want me to work
    for someone else, would you, somewhere else?

DISSON. I certainly wouldn't. You know what Wendy told me,
    don't you?

DIANA. What?

DISSON. She told me her last employer was always touching
    her.

WILLY. No?

DISSON. Always. Touching her.

DIANA. Her body, you mean?

DISSON. What else?

    Pause.

DIANA. Well, if we're to take it that that's general practice,
    I think it's safer to stay in the family, don't you? Mind you,
    they might not want to touch me in the way they wanted to
    touch her.

    Pause.

But, Robert, you must understand that I not only want to be your wife, but also your employee. I'm not embarrassing you, am I, Willy?

WILLY. No, of course you're not.

DIANA. Because by being your employee I can help to further your interests, our interests. That's what I want to do. And so does Willy, don't you?

Disson's office. Morning.

DISSON *alone. He stands in the centre of the room. He looks at the door, walks over to* WENDY'S *desk. He looks down at her deskchair. He touches it. Slowly, he sits in it. He sits still.*
The door opens. WENDY *comes in. He stands.*

DISSON. You're late.

WENDY. You were sitting in my chair, Mr Disson.

DISSON. I said you're late.

WENDY. I'm not at all.

    WENDY *walks to her desk.*
    DISSON *makes way for her. He moves across the room.*

I'm hurt.

DISSON. Why?

WENDY. I've put on my new dress.

    He turns, looks at her.

DISSON. When did you put it on?

WENDY. This morning.

    Pause.

DISSON. Where?

WENDY. In my flat.

DISSON. Which room?

WENDY. In the hall, actually. I have a long mirror in the hall.

    He stands looking at her.

Do you like it?

DISSON. Yes. Very nice.

Disson's house. Workroom.

DISSON. Hold it firmly. You're not holding it firmly.

> TOM *holds a length of wood on the table.* DISSON *chips at its base.*

Use pressure. Grip it.

JOHN. A clamp would be better.

DISSON. A clamp? I want you boys to learn how to concentrate your physical energies, to do something useful.

JOHN. What's it going to be, Dad?

DISSON. You'll find out.

> DISSON *chips. He straightens.*

Give me the saw.

JOHN. Me?

DISSON. The saw! Give me it! (*To* TOM.) What are you doing?

TOM. I'm holding this piece of wood.

DISSON. Well, stop it. I've finished chipping. Look at the point now.

JOHN. If you put some lead in there you could make a pencil out of it.

DISSON. They think you're very witty at your school, do they?

JOHN. Well, some do and some don't, actually, Dad.

DISSON. You. Take the saw.

TOM. Me?

DISSON. I want you to saw it off . . . from here.

> DISSON *makes a line with his finger on the wood.*

TOM. But I can't saw.

JOHN. What about our homework, Dad? We've got to write an essay about the Middle Ages.

DISSON. Never mind the Middle Ages.

JOHN. Never mind the *Middle Ages*?

TOM. Can't you demonstrate how to do it, Dad? Then we could watch.

DISSON. Oh, give me it.

DISSON *takes the saw and points to a mark on the wood.*
Now . . . from here.

TOM (*pointing*). You said from here.

DISSON. No, no, from here.

JOHN (*pointing to the other end*). I could have sworn you said from there.

Pause.

DISSON. Go to your room.

Pause.

Get out.

JOHN *goes out.* DISSON *looks at* TOM.

Do you want to learn anything?

TOM. Yes.

DISSON. Where did I say I was going to saw it?

He stares at the wood. TOM *holds it still.*

Hold it still. Hold it. Don't let it move.

DISSON *saws. The saw is very near* TOM'S *fingers.* TOM *looks down tensely.* DISSON *saws through.*

TOM. You nearly cut my fingers off.

DISSON. No, I didn't . . . I didn't . . .

He glares suddenly at TOM.

You didn't hold the wood still!

Disson's office.

The curtains are drawn.

DISSON. Come here. Put your chiffon round my eyes. My eyes hurt.

WENDY *ties a chiffon scarf round his eyes.*

I want you to make a call to Newcastle, to Mr Martin. We're still waiting for delivery of goods on Invoice No. 634729. What is the cause for delay?

WENDY *picks up the telephone, dials, waits.*

WENDY. Could I have Newcastle 77254, please. Thank you.

She waits. He touches her body.

Yes, I'm holding.

He touches her. She moves under his touch.

Hullo, Mr Martin, please. Mr Disson's office.

Camera on him. His arm stretching.

Mr Martin? Mr Disson's office. Mr Disson . . . Ah, you
know what it's about (*She laughs.*) Yes . . . Yes.

Camera on him. He leans forward, his arm stretching.

Oh, it's been dispatched? Oh good. Mr Disson will be glad.

She moves under his touch.

Oh, I will. Of course I will.

She puts the phone down. He withdraws his hand.

Mr Martin sends his apologies. The order has been dispatched.

The intercom buzzes. She switches through. WILLY'S *voice.*
Yes?

WILLY. Oh, Wendy, is Mr Disson there?

WENDY. Did you want to speak to him, Mr Torrance?

WILLY. No. Just ask him if I might borrow your services for
five minutes.

WENDY. Mr Torrance wants to know if he might borrow my
services for five minutes.

DISSON. What's happened to his own secretary?

WENDY. Mr Disson would like to know what has happened to
your own secretary.

WILLY. She's unwell. Gone home. Just five minutes, that's
all.

DISSON *gestures towards the door.*

WENDY. Be with you in a minute, Mr Torrance.

WILLY. Please thank Mr Disson for me.

The intercom switches off.

WENDY. Mr Torrance would like me to thank you for him.

DISSON. I heard.

WENDY *goes through the inner door into* WILLY'S *office,
shuts it.*

Silence.

DISSON *sits still, the chiffon round his eyes. He looks towards the door.*

He hears giggles, hissing, gurgles, squeals.

He goes to the door, squats by the handle, raises the chiffon, tries to look through the keyhole. Can see nothing through the keyhole. He drops the chiffon, puts his ear to the door. The handle presses into his skull. The sounds continue. Sudden silence.

The door has opened.

A pair of woman's legs stand by his squatting body.

He freezes, slowly puts forward a hand, touches a leg. He tears the chiffon from his eyes. It hangs from his neck. He looks up.

DIANA *looks down at him.*

Behind her, in the other room, WENDY *is sitting, taking dictation from* WILLY, *who is standing.*

DIANA. What game is this?

He remains.

Get up. What are you doing? What are you doing with that scarf? Get up from the floor. What are you doing?

DISSON. Looking for something.

DIANA. What?

WILLY *walks to the door, smiles, closes the door.*

What were you looking for? Get up.

DISSON (*standing*). Don't speak to me like that. How dare you speak to me like that? I'll knock your teeth out.

She covers her face.

What were you doing in there? I thought you'd gone home. What were you doing in there?

DIANA. I came back.

DISSON. You mean you were in there with both of them? In there with both of them?

DIANA. Yes! So what?

Pause.

DISSON (*calmly*). I was looking for my pencil, which had rolled

off my desk. Here it is. I found it, just before you came in,
and put it in my pocket. My eyes hurt. I borrowed Wendy's
scarf, to calm my eyes. Why are you getting so excited?

Disson's office. Day.
DISSON *at his desk, writing.* WENDY *walks to the cabinet,
examines a file. Silence.*
DISSON. What kind of flat do you have, Wendy?
WENDY. Quite a small one, Mr Disson. Quite pleasant.
DISSON. Not too big for you, then? Too lonely?
WENDY. Oh no, it's quite small. Quite cosy.
DISSON. Bathroom fittings any good?
WENDY. Adequate, Mr Disson. Not up to our standard.
  Pause.
DISSON. Live there alone, do you?
WENDY. No, I share it with a girl friend. But she's away quite
  a lot of the time. She's an air hostess. She wants me to become
  one, as a matter of fact.
DISSON. Listen to me, Wendy. Don't ever . . . dream of
  becoming an air hostess. Never. The glamour may dazzle
  from afar, but, believe you me, it's a mess of a life . . . a
  mess of a life . . .
  He watches WENDY *walk to her desk with a file and then
  back to the cabinet.*
  Were you lonely as a child?
WENDY. No.
DISSON. Nor was I. I had quite a lot of friends. True friends.
  Most of them live abroad now, of course – banana planters,
  oil engineers, Jamaica, the Persian Gulf . . . but if I were
  to meet them tomorrow, you know . . . just like that . . .
  there'd be no strangeness, no awkwardness at all. We'd
  continue where we left off, quite naturally.
  WENDY *bends low at the cabinet.*
  He stares at her buttocks.

It's a matter of a core of affection, you see . . . a core of
undying affection . . .

Suddenly WENDY'S *body appears in enormous close-up. Her
buttocks fill the screen.*
His hands go up to keep them at bay.
His elbow knocks a round table lighter from his desk.
Picture normal.
WENDY *turns from the cabinet, stands upright.*

WENDY. What was that?

DISSON. My lighter.

She goes to his desk.

WENDY. Where is it?

She kneels, looks under the desk. The lighter is at his feet.
She reaches for it. He kicks it across the room.

(*Laughing.*) Oh, Mr Disson, why did you do that?

*She stands. He stands. She goes towards the lighter. He gets
to it before her, stands with it at his feet. He looks at her.*
She stops.

What's this?

DISSON *feints his body, left to right*

DISSON. Come on.

WENDY. What?

DISSON. Tackle me. Get the ball.

WENDY. What do I tackle with?

DISSON. Your feet.

She moves forward deliberately.
*He dribbles away, turns, kicks the lighter along the carpet
towards her. Her foot stops the lighter. She turns with it at
her foot.*

Ah!

*She stands, legs apart, the lighter between them, staring at
him.*
She taps her foot.

WENDY. Come on, then!

He goes towards her. She eludes him. He grasps her arm.

That's a foul!

He drops her arm.

DISSON. Sorry.

She stands with the lighter between her feet.

WENDY. Come on, come on. Tackle me, tackle me. Come on, tackle me! Get the ball! Fight for the ball!

He begins to move, stops, sinks to the floor. She goes to him. What's the matter?

DISSON. Nothing. All right. Nothing.

WENDY. Let me help you up.

DISSON. No. Stay. You're very valuable in this office. Good worker. Excellent. If you have any complaints, just tell me. I'll soon put them right. You're a very efficient secretary. Something I've always needed. Have you everything you want? Are your working conditions satisfactory?

WENDY. Perfectly.

DISSON. Oh good. Good . . . Good.

Disson's house. Bedroom. Night

DISSON *and* DIANA *in bed, reading. She looks at him.*

DIANA. You seem a little subdued . . . lately.

DISSON. Me? Not at all. I'm reading the Life of Napoleon, that's all.

DIANA. No, I don't mean now, I mean generally. Is there – ?

DISSON. I'm not at all subdued. Really.

Pause.

DIANA. It's our first anniversary next Wednesday, did you know that?

DISSON. Of course I did. How could I forget? We'll go out together in the evening. Just you and I. Alone.

DIANA. Oh. Good.

DISSON. I'm also giving a little tea party in the office, in the afternoon. My mother and father'll be up.

DIANA. Oh good.

Pause.

DISSON. How have you enjoyed our first year?

DIANA. It's been wonderful. It's been a very exciting year.

Pause.

DISSON. You've been marvellous with the boys.

DIANA. They like me.

DISSON. Yes, they do. They do.

Pause.

It's been a great boon, to have you work for the firm.

DIANA. Oh, I'm glad. I am glad.

Pause.

Be nice to get away to Spain.

Pause.

DISSON. You've got enough money, haven't you? I mean, you have sufficient money to see you through, for all you want?

DIANA. Oh yes. I have, thank you.

Pause.

DISSON. I'm very proud of you, you know.

DIANA. I'm proud of you.

Silence.

Disson's office.

DISSON. Have you written to Corley?

WENDY. Yes, Mr Disson.

DISSON. And Turnbull?

WENDY. Yes, Mr Disson.

DISSON. And Erverley?

WENDY. Yes, Mr Disson.

DISSON. Carbon of the Erverley letter, please.

WENDY. Here you are, Mr Disson.

DISSON. Ah. I see you've spelt Erverley right.

WENDY. Right?

DISSON. People tend, very easily, to leave out the first R and call him Everley. You haven't done that.

WENDY. No. (*She turns.*)

DISSON. Just a minute. How did you spell Turnbull? You needn't show me. Tell me.

WENDY. TURNBULL.

DISSON. Quite correct.

    Pause.

    Quite correct. Now what about – ?

      The screen goes black.

    Where are you?

      Pause.

    I can't see you.

WENDY. I'm here, Mr Disson.

DISSON. Where?

WENDY. You're looking at me, Mr Disson.

DISSON. You mean my eyes are open?

      Pause.

WENDY. I'm where I was. I haven't moved.

DISSON. Are my eyes open?

WENDY. Mr Disson, really . . .

DISSON. Is this you? This I feel?

WENDY. Yes.

DISSON. What, all this I can feel?

WENDY. You're playing one of your games, Mr Disson. You're being naughty again.

    Vision back.

    DISSON *looks at her.*

    You sly old thing.

Disley's surgery.

A torch shines in DISSON'S *eyes, first right, then left. Torch out.*
Light on.

DISLEY. There's nothing wrong with them.

DISSON. What then?

DISLEY. I only deal with eyes, old chap. Why do you come to me? Why don't you go to someone else?

DISSON. Because it's my eyes that are affected.

DISLEY. Look. Why don't you go to someone else?

DISLEY begins to clear away his instruments.

Nothing worrying you, is there?

DISSON. Of course not. I've got everything I want.

DISLEY. Getting a holiday soon?

DISSON. Going to Spain.

DISLEY. Lucky man.

Pause.

DISSON. Look. Listen. You're my oldest friend. You were going to be the best man at my wedding.

DISLEY. That's right.

DISSON. You wrote a wonderful speech in my honour.

DISLEY. Yes.

DISSON. But you were ill. You had to opt out.

DISLEY. That's right.

Pause.

DISSON. Help me.

Pause.

DISLEY. Who made the speech? Your brother-in-law, wasn't it?

DISSON. I don't want you to think I'm not a happy man. I am.

DISLEY. What sort of speech did he make?

Disson's house. Sitting-room. Evening.

DISSON. Tell me about Sunderley.

WILLY. Sunderley?

DISSON. Tell me about the place where you two were born. Where you played at being brother and sister.

WILLY. We didn't have to play at being brother and sister. We were brother and sister.

DIANA. Stop drinking.

DISSON. Drinking? You call this drinking? This? I used to down eleven or nine pints a night! Eleven or nine pints! Every night of the stinking week! Me and the boys! The boys! And me! I'd break any man's hand for . . . for playing me false. That was before I became a skilled craftsman. That was before . . .

    He falls silent, sits.

WILLY. Sunderley was beautiful.

DISSON. I know.

WILLY. And now it's gone, for ever.

DISSON. I never got there.

    DISSON *stands, goes to get a drink.*

    He turns from drinks table.

What are you whispering about? Do you think I don't hear? Think I don't see? I've got my memories, too. Long before this.

WILLY. Yes, Sunderley was beautiful.

DISSON. The lake.

WILLY. The lake.

DISSON. The long windows.

WILLY. From the withdrawing-room.

DISSON. On to the terrace.

WILLY. Music playing.

DISSON. On the piano.

WILLY. The summer nights. The wild swans.

DISSON. What swans? What bloody swans?

WILLY. The owls.

DISSON. Negroes at the gate, under the trees.

WILLY. No Negroes.

DISSON. Why not?

WILLY. We had no Negroes.

DISSON. Why in God's name not?

WILLY. Just one of those family quirks, Robert.

DIANA (*standing*). Robert.

    Pause.

Come to bed.

DISSON. You can say that, in front of him?

DIANA. Please.

DISSON. In front of *him*?

He goes to her.

Why did you marry me?

DIANA. I admired you. You were so positive.

DISSON. You loved me.

DIANA. You were kind.

DISSON. You loved me for that?

DIANA. I found you admirable in your clarity of mind, your surety of purpose, your will, the strength your achievements had given you –

DISSON. And you adored me for it?

WILLY (*to* DISSON). Can I have a private word with you?

DISSON. You *adored* me for it?

Pause.

DIANA. You know I did.

WILLY. Can I have a private word with you, old chap? (*To* DIANA.) Please.

DIANA *goes out of the room.*

DISSON *looks at* WILLY.

DISSON. Mind how you tread, Bill. Mind . . . how you tread, old Bill, old boy, old Bill.

WILLY. Listen. I've been wondering. Is there anything on your mind?

DISSON. My mind? No, of course not.

WILLY. You're not dissatisfied with my work, or anything?

DISSON. Quite the contrary. Absolutely the contrary.

WILLY. Oh good. I like the work very much. Try to do my best.

DISSON. Listen. I want you to be my partner. Hear me? I want you to share full responsibility . . . with me.

WILLY. Do you really?

DISSON. Certainly.

WILLY. Well, thank you very much. I don't know what to say.
DISSON. Don't say anything.

Disson's office.
WILLY *at the door.*
WILLY. Coming, old chap?
DISSON. Yes.
WILLY (*to* WENDY). Important lunch, this. But I think we'll
   swing it, don't you, Robert? (*To* WENDY.) Great prospects
   in store.

> DISSON *and* WILLY *go out.* WENDY *clips some papers
> together.*

> DIANA *comes in through the inner door.*

WENDY. Oh, hullo, Mrs Disson.
DIANA. Hullo, Wendy.
   Pause.
   DIANA *watches* WENDY *clip the papers.*
Do you like being a secretary?
WENDY. I do, yes. Do you?
DIANA. I do, yes.
   Pause.
I understand your last employer touched your body . . .
rather too much.
WENDY. It wasn't a question of too much, Mrs Disson. One
   touch was enough for me.
DIANA. Oh, you left after the first touch?
WENDY. Well, not quite the first, no.
   Pause.
DIANA. Have you ever asked yourself why men will persist in
   touching women?
WENDY. No, I've never asked myself that, Mrs Disson.
DIANA. Few women do ask themselves that question.
WENDY. Don't they? I don't know. I've never spoken to any
   other women on the subject.

DIANA. You're speaking to me.

WENDY. Yes. Well, have you ever asked yourself that question, Mrs Disson?

DIANA. Never. No.

Pause.

Have lunch with me today. Tell me about yourself.

WENDY. I'll have lunch with you with pleasure.

DISSON *comes in. They look at him. He at them. Silence.*

DISSON. Forgotten . . . one of the designs.

DIANA *smiles at him.* WENDY *clips her papers. He goes to his desk, collects a folder, stands upright.*

DIANA *looks out of the window.* WENDY *clips papers. He looks at them, goes out.* DIANA *and* WENDY *remain silent.*

Disson's house. Games room.

DISSON *and* WILLY *playing ping-pong. They are in the middle of a long rally.* THE TWINS *watch.* WILLY *is on the attack,* DISSON *playing desperately, retrieving from positions of great difficulty. He cuts, chops, pushes.*

TWINS (*variously*). Well done, Dad. Good shot, Dad. Good one, Dad.

WILLY *forces* DISSON *on to the forehand. He slams viciously.*

DISSON *skids.*

The screen goes black.

Good shot!

DISSON. Aaah!

Vision back.

DISSON *is clutching the table, bent over it.*

WILLY *throws the ball on to the table.*

It bounces gently across it.

Disson's house. Sitting-room. Evening.

DISSON'S *parents.*

MOTHER. Have I seen that mirror before?

DISSON. No. It's new.

MOTHER. I knew I hadn't seen it. Look at it, John. What a beautiful mirror.

FATHER. Must have cost you a few bob.

MOTHER. Can you see the work on it, John? I bet it must be a few years old, that mirror.

DISSON. It's a few hundred years old.

FATHER. I bet it must have cost you a few bob.

DISSON. It wasn't cheap.

FATHER. Cheap?

MOTHER. What a beautiful mirror.

FATHER. Cheap? Did you hear what he said, Dora? He said it wasn't cheap!

MOTHER. No, I bet it wasn't.

FATHER (*laughing*). Cheap!
    Pause.

MOTHER. Mrs Tidy sends you her love.

DISSON. Who?

FATHER. Mrs Tidy. The Tidys.

DISSON. Oh yes. How are they?

FATHER. Still very tidy. (*Laughs.*) Aren't they, Dora?

MOTHER. You remember the Tidys.

DISSON. Of course I remember them.
    Pause.

How have you been keeping, then?

FATHER. Oh, your mother's had a few pains. You know, just a few.

MOTHER. Only a few, John. I haven't had many pains.

FATHER. I only said you'd had a few. Not many.
    Pause.

MOTHER. Are the boys looking forward to their holiday?

DISSON. Yes, they are.

FATHER. When are you going?

DISSON. I'm not.

Disson's office.

DISSON. Tighter.

    WENDY *ties the chiffon round his eyes.*

WENDY. There. You look nice.

DISSON. This chiffon stinks.

WENDY. Oh, I do apologize. What of?

    Pause.

You're very rude to me. But you do look nice. You really do.

    DISSON *tears the chiffon off.*

DISSON. It's useless. Ring Disley. Tell him to come here.

WENDY. But he'll be here at four o'clock, for your tea party.

DISSON. I want him now! I want him . . . now.

WENDY. Don't you like my chiffon any more, to put round your eyes? My lovely chiffon?

    Pause.

    He sits still.

I always feel like kissing you when you've got that on round your eyes. Do you know that? Because you're all in the dark.

    Pause.

Put it on.

    She picks up the chiffon and folds it.

I'll put it on . . . for you. Very gently.

    She leans forward.

    He touches her.

No – you mustn't touch me, if you're not wearing your chiffon.

    She places the chiffon on his eyes.

    He trembles, puts his hand to the chiffon, slowly lowers it, lets it fall.

    It flutters to the floor.

    As she looks at him, he reaches for the telephone.

Disson's office.

DISSON *in the same position.*

DISSON. I need a tight bandage. Very tight.

DISLEY. Anyone could do that for you.

DISSON. No. You're my eye consultant. You must do it for
me.

DISLEY. All right.

> *He takes a bandage from his case and ties it round* DISSON'S
> *eyes.*

Just for half an hour. You don't want it on when your guests
arrive, do you?

> DISLEY *ties the knots.*

This'll keep you in the dark, all right. Also lend pressure to
your temples. Is that what you want?

DISSON. That's it. That's what I want.

> DISLEY *cuts the strands.*

DISLEY. There. How's that?

> *Pause.*

See anything?

Disson's office. Afternoon.

DISSON *sits alone, the bandage round his eyes.*

Silence.

WILLY *enters from his office. He sees* DISSON *and goes to him.*

WILLY. How are you, old chap? Bandage on straight? Knots
tight?

> *He pats him on the back and goes out through the front office
> door.*
> *The door slams.*
> DISSON *sits still.*

Corridor.

MR *and* MRS DISLEY *approaching the office.*

LOIS. Why didn't he make it a cocktail party? Why a tea
   party, of all things?

DISLEY. I couldn't say.

Office.

DISSON'S *head.*

*Soft clicks of door opening and closing, muffled steps, an odd cough,
slight rattle of teacups.*

Corridor.

DISSON'S *parents approaching the office.*

MOTHER. I could do with a cup of tea, couldn't you, John?

Office.

DISSON'S *head.*

*Soft clicks of door opening and closing, muffled steps, an odd
cough, slight rattle of teacups.*

Corridor.

THE TWINS *approach, silent.*

Office.

DISSON'S *head.*

*Soft clicks of door opening and closing, muffled steps, an odd cough,
slight rattle of teacups, a short whisper.*

Corridor.

DIANA *and* WILLY *approach.*

DIANA. Why *don't* you come to Spain with us?

WILLY. I think I will.

Office.
DISSON'S *head.*
Soft clicks of door opening and closing, muffled steps, an odd cough,
slight rattle of teacups, whispers.

Corridor.
WENDY *approaches.*

Office.
DISSON'S *head.*
Soft clicks of door opening and closing, muffled steps, an odd cough,
slight rattle of teacups, whispers.

Office.
A buffet table has been set out. Two ELDERLY LADIES *serve*
tea, sandwiches, bridge rolls, buns and cakes. The gathering is
grouped around the table in silence. DISLEY *whispers to them.*
DISLEY. His eyes are a little strained, that's all. Just resting
    them. Don't mention it. It'll embarrass him. It's quite all
    right.
        They all take their tea, choose edibles, and relax.
JOHN (*choosing a cake*). These are good.
TOM. What are they?
DIANA (*choosing a bridge roll*). These look nice.
LOIS. You look wonderful, Mrs Disson. Absolutely wonderful.
    Doesn't she, Peter?
DISLEY. Marvellous.
LOIS. What do you think of your grandsons?
FATHER. They've grown up now, haven't they?

LOIS. Of course, we knew them when they were that high, didn't we, Tom?

FATHER. So did we.

TOM. Yes.

WILLY. Big lads now, aren't they, these two?

JOHN. Cake, Granny?

MOTHER. No, I've had one.

JOHN. Have two.

FATHER. I'll have one.

MOTHER. He's had one.

FATHER. I'll have two.

> WENDY *takes a cup of tea to* DISSON *and puts it into his hands.*

WENDY. Here's a cup of tea, Mr Disson. Drink it. It's warm.

LOIS (*to* DIANA). You're off to Spain quite soon, aren't you, Diana?

DIANA. Yes, quite soon.

DISLEY (*calling*). We'll take off those bandages in a minute, old chap!

LOIS. Spain is wonderful at this time of the year.

WILLY. Any time of the year, really.

LOIS. But I think it's best at this time of the year, don't you?

DIANA. What sun lotion do you use, Lois?

DISSON'S *point of view.*
No dialogue is heard in all shots from DISSON'S *point of view. Silence.*
Figures mouthing silently, in conspiratorial postures, seemingly whispering together.

Shot including DISSON.

TOM. I went into goal yesterday.

WILLY. How did you do?

LOIS. You can get it anywhere. It's perfect.

JOHN. He made two terrific saves.

TOM. The first was a fluke.

LOIS. How do you sun, then?

DIANA. I have to be rather careful.

TOM. Second save wasn't a bad save.

LOIS. How do you sun, Wendy?

WENDY. Oh not too bad, really.

LOIS (*to* MRS DISSON). We go to our little island every year and when we go we have to leave our poor little Siamese with my mother.

MOTHER. Do you really?

LOIS. They're almost human, aren't they, Siamese?

DIANA. I'm sure my Siamese was.

LOIS. Aren't they, Peter, almost human?

DIANA. Wasn't Tiger a human cat, Willy, at Sunderley?

WILLY. He adored you.

DISLEY. They really are almost human, aren't they, Siamese?

DISSON'S *point of view.*

Silence.

The party splits into groups. Each group whispering.

The two ELDERLY LADIES *at the buffet table.*

DISSON'S PARENTS, *sitting together.*

THE TWINS *and the* DISLEYS.

WILLY, WENDY *and* DIANA *in a corner.*

Shot including DISSON.

The gathering in a close group, the PARENTS *sitting.*

LOIS. I'd go like a shot.

WENDY. What, me? Come to Spain?

DIANA. Yes, why not?

    WILLY *leans across* DISLEY.

WILLY. Yes, of course you must come. Of course you must come.
WENDY. How wonderful.

DISSON'S *point of view.*
WILLY *approaches* DISSON. *With a smile, he takes a ping-pong ball from his pocket, and puts it into* DISSON'S *hand.*
DISSON *clutches it.*

DISSON'S *point of view.*
WILLY *returns to* WENDY *and* DIANA, *whispers to them.*
DIANA *laughs (silently), head thrown back, gasps with laughter.*
WENDY *smiles.*
WILLY *puts one arm round* WENDY, *the other round* DIANA.
He leads them to WENDY'S *desk.*
WILLY *places cushions on the desk.*
DIANA *and* WENDY, *giggling silently, hoist themselves up on to the desk. They lie head to toe.*

DISSON'S *point of view. Close-up.*
WENDY'S *face.* WILLY'S *fingers caressing it.* DIANA'S *shoes in background.*

DISSON'S *point of view. Close-up.*
DIANA'S *face.* WILLY'S *fingers caressing it.* WENDY'S *shoes in background.*

DISSON'S *point of view.*
LOIS *powdering her nose.*

DISSON'S *point of view.*
The ELDERLY LADIES *drinking tea, at the table.*

DISSON'S *point of view.*
DISLEY *talking to the boys by the window.* THE TWINS *listening intently.*

DISSON'S *point of view.*
DISSON'S PARENTS *sitting, dozing.*

DISSON'S *point of view.*
The base of WENDY'S *desk.*
A shoe drops to the floor.

Shot including DISSON.
DISSON *falls to the floor in his chair with a crack. His teacup drops and spills.*
The gathering is grouped by the table, turns.
DISLEY *and* WILLY *go to him.*
They try to lift him from the chair, are unable to do so.
DISLEY *cuts the bandage and takes it off.*
DISSON'S *eyes are open.*
DISLEY *feels his pulse.*
DISLEY. He's all right. Get him up.
> DISLEY *and* WILLY *try to pull him up from the chair, are unable to do so.*
> JOHN *and* TOM *join them.*
Get it up.

The four of them, with great effort, manage to set the chair on its feet.

DISSON *is still seated.*

He must lie down. Now, two hold the chair, and two pull him.

    JOHN *and* WILLY *hold the chair.*

    DISLEY *and* TOM *pull.*

The chair.
The chair scrapes, moves no farther.

The group around the chair.
They pull, with great effort.

The chair.
The chair scrapes, moves no farther.

The room.

WILLY. Anyone would think he was chained to it!

DISLEY (*pulling*). Come out!

MOTHER. Bobbie!

    They stop pulling.

    DISSON *in the chair, still, his eyes open.*

    DIANA *comes to him.*

    She kneels by him.

DIANA. This is . . . Diana.

    Pause.

  Can you hear me?

    Pause.

  Can he see me?

    Pause.

Robert.
Pause.
Can you hear me?
Pause.
Robert, can you see me?
Pause.
It's me. It's me, darling.
Slight pause.
It's your wife.

DISSON'S *face in close-up.*
DISSON'S *eyes. Open.*

THE BASEMENT

The Basement was first presented by B.B.C. Television on 20 February 1967 with the following cast:

STOTT   Harold Pinter

JANE   Kika Markham

LAW   Derek Godfrey

Directed by Charles Jarrott

THE BASEMENT

Exterior. Front area of a basement flat.
Winter. Night.
Rain falling.
Short stone flight of steps from street.
Light shining through the basement door.
The upper part of the house is dark.
The back of a man, STOTT. *He stands in the centre of the area,*
looking towards the door.
He wears a raincoat, his head is bare.

Exterior. Front area.
STOTT'S *face. Behind him, by the wall, a girl,* JANE. *She is*
huddled by the wall. She wears a rainhat, clasps her raincoat to
her.

Interior. Room.
The room is large and long. A window at one end looks out to a
small concrete yard. There are doors to bathroom and kitchen.
The room is comfortable, relaxed, heavily furnished.
Numerous side tables, plants, arm-chairs, book-cabinets, book-
shelves, velvet cloths, a desk, paintings, a large double bed. There
is a large fire in the grate.
The room is lit by a number of table and standard lamps.
LAW *is lying low in an arm-chair, reading, by the fireside.*
Silence.

Exterior. Front area.
STOTT *still.*

Interior. Room.
LAW *in arm-chair. He is smiling at his book.*
He giggles. He is reading a Persian love manual, with illustrations.

Exterior. Front area.
JANE *huddled by the wall.*
STOTT *moves to the door.*

Interior. Room.
Doorbell. LAW *looks up from his book. He closes it, puts it on a side table, goes into the hall.*

Interior. Small hall.
LAW *approaches the front door. He opens it.*
Silence.
He stares at STOTT. *From his position in the doorway* LAW *cannot see the girl.*
LAW (*with great pleasure*). Stott!
STOTT (*smiling*). Hullo, Tim.
LAW. Good God. Come in!
    LAW *laughs.*
  Come in!
    STOTT *enters.*
  I can't believe it!

Interior. Room.
LAW *and* STOTT *enter.*
LAW. Give me your coat. You're soaking. Come on. That's it.
  I'm absolutely flabbergasted. You must be freezing.
STOTT. I am a bit.
LAW. Go on, warm yourself. Warm yourself by the fire.

STOTT. Thanks.

LAW. Sit down by the fire. Go on.

STOTT *moves to the fire.*

LAW *takes the coat into hall.*

Interior. Hall.

LAW *comes into the hall, shaking the raincoat. He looks inside it, at the label, smiles. He hangs it on a hook.*

Interior. Room.

STOTT *warming his hands at the fire.* LAW *comes in.*

LAW. You haven't changed at all. You haven't changed . . . at all!

STOTT *laughs.*

You've got a new raincoat though. Oh yes, I noticed. Hold on, I'll get you a towel.

LAW *goes to the bathroom.*

STOTT, *alone, looks up and about him at the room.*

Interior. Room.

The room.

Interior. Bathroom.

LAW *in bathroom, at the airing cupboard. He swiftly throws aside a number of towels, chooses a soft one with a floral pattern.*

Interior. Room.

LAW *comes in with a towel.*

LAW. Here's a towel. Go on, give it a good wipe. That's it.

You didn't walk here, did you? You're soaking. What happened to your car? You could have driven here. Why didn't you give me a ring? But how did you know my address? My God, it's years. If you'd have rung I would have picked you up. I would have picked you up in my car. What happened to your car?

> STOTT *finishes drying his hair, puts the towel on the arm of a chair.*

STOTT. I got rid of it.

LAW. But how are you? Are you well? You look well.

STOTT. How are you?

LAW. Oh, I'm well. Just a minute, I'll get you some slippers.

> LAW *goes to the cupboard, bends.*

You're going to stay the night, aren't you? You'll have to, look at the time. I wondered if you'd ever turn up again. Really. For years. Here you are. Here's some slippers.

STOTT. Thanks.

> STOTT *takes the slippers, changes his shoes.*

LAW. I'll find some pyjamas in a minute. Still, we'll have a cup of coffee first, or some . . . Or a drink? What about a drink?

STOTT. Ah.

> LAW *pours drinks, brings the drinks to the sofa and sits down by* STOTT.

LAW. You're not living at Chatsworth Road any more, are you? I know that. I've passed by there, numbers of times. You've moved. Where are you living now?

STOTT. I'm looking for a place.

LAW. Stay here! Stay here as long as you like. I've got another bed I can fit up. I've got a camp bed I can fit up.

STOTT. I don't want to impose upon you.

LAW. Not a bit, not a bit.

> *Pause.*

STOTT. Oh, by the way, I've got a friend outside. Can she come in?

LAW. A friend?

STOTT. Outside.

LAW. A friend? Outside?

STOTT. Can she come in?

LAW. Come in? Yes . . . yes . . . of course . . .

    STOTT *goes towards the door.*

  What's she doing outside?

Exterior. Front door.

JANE *is standing in the narrow porch outside the door.*
The door opens.

Interior. Room.

LAW. STOTT *brings the girl in.*

STOTT. This is Jane. This is Tim Law.

    She smiles.

JANE. It's kind of you.

LAW. How do you do? I . . . must get you a towel.

JANE. No, thank you. My hair was covered.

LAW. But your face?

    STOTT *comes forward.*

STOTT. It's very kind of you, Tim. It really is. Here's a towel.
 (*He gives it to her.*) Here.

LAW. But that's your towel.

JANE. I don't mind, really.

LAW. I have clean ones, dry ones.

JANE (*patting her face*). This is clean.

LAW. But it's not dry.

JANE. It's very soft.

LAW. I have others.

JANE. There. I'm dry.

LAW. You can't be.

JANE. What a splendid room.

STOTT. Isn't it? A little bright, perhaps.

LAW. Too much light?

STOTT *turns a lamp off.*

STOTT. Do you mind?

LAW. No.

JANE *begins to take her clothes off.*

In the background STOTT *moves about the room, turning off the lamps.*

LAW *stands still.*

STOTT *turns off all the lamps but one, by the fireside.*

JANE, *naked, gets into the bed.*

Can I get you some cocoa? Some hot chocolate?

STOTT *takes his clothes off and, naked, gets into the bed.*

I was feeling quite lonely, actually. It is lonely sitting here, night after night. Mind you, I'm very happy here. Remember that place we shared? That awful place in Chatsworth Road? I've come a long way since then. I bought this flat cash down. It's mine. I don't suppose you've noticed the hi-fi stereo? There's all sorts of things I can show you.

LAW *unbuttons his cardigan.*

He places it over the one lit lamp, so shading the light. He sits by the fire.

The lamp covered by the cardigan.

Patch of light on the ceiling.

Patch of light at LAW'S *feet.*

LAW'S *hands on the chair arms.*

A gasp from JANE.

LAW'S *hands do not move.*

LAW'S *legs. Beyond them, the fire almost dead.*

LAW *puts on his glasses.*

LAW *reaches for* The Persian Manual of Love.

LAW *peers to read.*
A long sigh from JANE.
LAW *reads.*

Exterior. Cliff-top. Day. Summer.
Long-shot of STOTT *standing on a cliff-top.*

Exterior. Beach.
The beach is long and deserted. LAW *and* JANE, *in swimming costumes.* JANE *building a sandcastle.* LAW *watches her.*

LAW. How old are you?

JANE. I'm very young.

LAW. You are young.

> *He watches her work.*

You're a child.

> *He watches her.*

Have you known him long?

JANE. No.

LAW. I have. Charming man. Man of great gifts. Very old friend of mine, as a matter of fact. Has he told you?

JANE. No.

LAW. You don't know him very well?

JANE. No.

LAW. He has a connexion with the French aristocracy. He was educated in France. Speaks French fluently, of course. Have you read his French translations?

JANE. No.

LAW. Ah. They're immaculate. Great distinction. Formidable scholar, Stott. Do you know what he got at Oxford? He got a First in Sanskrit at Oxford. A First in Sanskrit!

JANE. How wonderful.

LAW. You never knew?

JANE. Never.

LAW. I know for a fact he owns three chateâux. Three superb châteaux. Have you ever ridden in his Alvis? His Facel Vega? What an immaculate driver. Have you seen his yachts? Huh! What yachts. What yachts.

    JANE *completes her sandcastle.*

How pleased I was to see him. After so long. One loses touch . . . so easily.

Interior. Cave. Day.
STOTT'S *body lying in the sand, asleep.*
LAW *and* JANE *appear at the mouth of the cave. They arrive at the body, look down.*
LAW. What repose he has.
STOTT'S *body in the sand.*
Their shadows across him.

Interior. Room. Night.
LAW *lying on the floor, a cushion at his head, covered by a blanket. His eyes are closed.*
Silence.
A long gasp from JANE.
LAW'S *eyes open.*

STOTT *and* JANE *in bed.*
STOTT *turning to wall.*
JANE *turns to the edge of the bed.*
She leans over the edge of the bed and smiles at LAW.

LAW *looks at her.*

JANE *smiles.*

Interior. Room. Day.
STOTT *lifts a painting from the wall, looks at it.*
STOTT. No.
LAW. No, you're quite right. I've never liked it.

> STOTT *walks across room to a second picture, looks at it. He turns to look at* LAW.

No.

> STOTT *takes it down and turns to look at the other paintings.*
All of them. All of them. You're right. They're terrible. Take them down.

> *The paintings are all similar watercolours.*
> STOTT *begins to take them from the walls.*

Interior. Kitchen. Day.
JANE *in the kitchen, cooking at the stove, humming.*

Exterior. Backyard. Winter. Day.
The yard is surrounded by high blank walls.

STOTT *and* LAW *sitting at an iron table, with a pole for an umbrella.*

They are drinking lager.

LAW. Who is she? Where did you meet her?

STOTT. She's charming, isn't she?

LAW. Charming. A little young.

STOTT. She comes from a rather splendid family, actually.

LAW. Really?

STOTT. Rather splendid.

> *Pause.*

LAW. Very helpful, of course, around the house.

STOTT. Plays the harp, you know.

LAW. Well?

STOTT. Remarkably well.

LAW. What a pity I don't possess one. You don't possess a harp, do you?

STOTT. Of course I possess a harp.

LAW. A recent acquisition?

STOTT. No, I've had it for years.

> *Pause.*

LAW. You don't find she's lacking in maturity?

Exterior. Beach. Summer. Day.

LAW *and* JANE *lying in the sand.* JANE *caressing him.*

JANE (*whispering*). Yes, yes, yes; oh you are, oh you are, oh you are . . .

LAW. We can be seen.

JANE. Why do you resist? How can you resist?

LAW. We can be seen! Damn you!

Exterior. Backyard. Winter. Day.

STOTT *and* LAW *at the table with lager.*

JANE *comes to the back door.*

JANE. Lunch is up!

Interior. Hall. Day.
LAW *and* JANE *come in at the front door with towels over their shoulders.*

Interior. Room. Day. Summer.
LAW *and* JANE *at the entrance of the room, towels over their shoulders, staring at the room.*
The room is unrecognizable. The furnishing has changed. There are Scandinavian tables and desks. Large bowls of Swedish glass. Tubular chairs. An Indian rug. Parquet floors, shining. A new hi-fi cabinet, etc. Fireplace blocked. The bed is the same.
STOTT *is at the window, closing the curtains. He turns.*
STOTT. Have a good swim?

Interior. Room. Night. Winter. (Second furnishing.)
STOTT *and* JANE *in bed, smoking.* LAW *sitting.*
STOTT. Let's have some music. We haven't heard your hi-fi for ages. Let's hear your stereo. What are you going to play?

Interior. Bar. Evening.
Large empty bar. All the tables unoccupied.
STOTT, LAW *and* JANE *at one table.*
STOTT. This was one of our old haunts, wasn't it, Tim? This was one of our haunts. Tim was always my greatest friend, you know. Always. It's marvellous. I've found my old friend again –
    Looking at JANE.
And discovered a new. And you like each other so much. It's really very warming.
LAW. Same again? (*To* WAITER.) Same again. (*To* JANE.)

Same again? (*To* WAITER.) Same again. The same again, all round. Exactly the same.

STOTT. I'll change to Campari.

LAW (*clicking his fingers at the* WAITER). One Campari here. Otherwise the same again.

STOTT. Remember those nights reading Proust? Remember them?

LAW (*to* JANE). In the original.

STOTT. The bouts with Laforgue? What bouts.

LAW. I remember.

STOTT. The great elms they had then. The great elm trees.

LAW. And the poplars.

STOTT. The cricket. The squash courts. You were pretty hot stuff at squash, you know.

LAW. You were unbeatable.

STOTT. Your style was deceptive.

LAW. It still is.

    LAW *laughs.*

  It still is!

STOTT. Not any longer.

    The WAITER *serves the drinks.*

    Silence. STOTT *lifts his glass.*

  Yes, I really am a happy man.

Exterior. Field. Evening. Winter.

STOTT *and* LAW. JANE *one hundred yards across the field.*

She holds a scarf.

LAW (*shouting*). Hold the scarf up. When you drop it, we run.

    She holds the scarf up.

    LAW *rubs his hands.* STOTT *looks at him.*

STOTT. Are you quite sure you want to do this?

LAW. Of course I'm sure.

JANE. On your marks!

    STOTT *and* LAW *get on their marks.*

Get set!

> *They get set.*
> JANE *drops scarf.*

Go!

> LAW *runs.* STOTT *stays still.*
> LAW, *going fast, turns to look for* STOTT; *off balance, stumbles, falls, hits his chin on the ground.*
> *Lying flat, he looks back at* STOTT.

LAW. Why didn't you run?

Exterior. Field.
JANE *stands, scarf in her hand. Downfield,* STOTT *stands.*
LAW *lies on the grass.* LAW'S *voice:*
LAW. Why didn't you run?

Interior. Room. Night. Winter. (Second furnishing.)
STOTT. Let's have some music. We haven't heard your hi-fi for ages.

> STOTT *opens the curtains and the window.*
> *Moonlight.* LAW *and* JANE *sit in chairs, clench their bodies with cold.*

Exterior. Backyard. Day. Winter.
STOTT *walking.* LAW, *wearing a heavy overcoat, collar turned up, watching him.* LAW *approaches him.*
LAW. Listen. Listen. I must speak to you. I must speak frankly. Listen. Don't you think it's a bit crowded in that flat, for the three of us?
STOTT. No, no. Not at all.
LAW. Listen, listen. Stop walking. Stop walking. Please. Wait.

> STOTT *stops.*

Listen. Wouldn't you say that the flat is a little small, for three people?

STOT T (*patting his shoulder*). No, no. Not at all.

STOTT *continues walking.*

LAW (*following him*). To look at it another way, to look at it another way, I can assure you that the Council would object strenuously to three people living in these conditions. The Town Council, I know for a fact, would feel it incumbent upon itself to register the strongest possible objections. And so would the Church.

STOTT *stops walking, looks at him.*

STOTT. Not at all. Not at all.

Interior. Room. Day. Summer.
The curtains are closed. The three at lunch, at the table. STOTT *and* JANE *are wearing tropical clothes.* JANE *is sitting on* STOTT'S *lap.*

LAW. Why don't we open the curtains?

STOTT *eats a grape.*

It's terribly close. Shall I open the window?

STOTT. What are you going to play? Debussy, I hope.

LAW *goes to the record cabinet. He examines record after record, feverishly, flings them one after the other at the wall.*

STOTT. Where's Debussy?

STOTT *kisses* JANE.

Another record hits the wall.

Where's Debussy? That's what we want. That's what we need. That's what we need at the moment.

JANE *breaks away from* STOTT *and goes out into the yard.*

STOTT *sits still.*

LAW. I've found it!

Interior. Room. Night. Winter.
LAW *turns with the record.*

The room is furnished as at the beginning.
STOTT *and* JANE, *naked, climb into bed.*
LAW *puts the record down and places his cardigan over the one lit lamp.*
He sits, picks up the poker and pokes the dying fire.

Exterior. Backyard. Day. Summer.
JANE *sitting at the iron table.*
STOTT *approaches her with a glass and bottle.*
He pours wine into the glass.
He bends over her, attempts to touch her breast.
She moves her body away from him.
STOTT *remains still.*

LAW *watches from the open windows.*
He moves to the table with the record and smiles at STOTT.
LAW. I've found the record. The music you wanted.
  STOTT *slams his glass on the table and goes into the room.*
  LAW *sits at the table, drinks from the bottle, regards* JANE.
  JANE *plays with a curl in her hair.*

Interior. Cave by the sea. Evening. Summer.
LAW *and* JANE. *He lying, she sitting, by him.*
She bends and whispers to him.
JANE. Why don't you tell him to go? We had such a lovely home. We had such a cosy home. It was so warm. Tell him to go. It's your place. Then we could be happy again. Like we used to. Like we used to. In our first blush of love. Then we could be happy again, like we used to. We could be happy again. Like we used to.

Exterior. Backyard. Night. Winter.
The yard is icy. The window is open. The room is lit.
LAW *is whispering to* STOTT *at the window. In the background*
JANE *sits sewing. (Second furnishing.)*

Exterior. Backyard. Window.
LAW *and* STOTT *at the open window,* STOTT'S *body hunched.*
LAW (*whispering very deliberately*). She betrays you. She betrays
    you. She has no loyalty. After all you've done for her. Shown
    her the world. Given her faith. You've been deluded. She's
    a savage. A viper. She sullies this room. She dirties this
    room. All this beautiful furniture. This beautiful Scandi-
    navian furniture. She dirties it. She sullies the room.
    STOTT *turns slowly to regard* JANE.

Interior. Room. Day.
The curtains are closed.
STOTT *in bed.* JANE *bending over him, touching his head.*
She looks across at LAW.
Silence. (Second furnishing.)
LAW. Is he breathing?
JANE. Just.
LAW. His last, do you think?
    Pause.
    Do you think it could be his last?
JANE. It could be.
LAW. How could it have happened? He seemed so fit. He was
    fit. As fit as a fiddle. Perhaps we should have called a doctor.
    And now he's dying. Are you heartbroken?
JANE. Yes.
LAW. So am I.
    Pause.
JANE. What shall we do with the body?

LAW. Body? He's not dead yet. Perhaps he'll recover.

> *They stare at each other.*

Interior. Room. Night.
LAW *and* JANE *in a corner, snuffling each other like animals.*

Interior. Room. Night.
STOTT *at the window. He opens the curtains. Moonlight pierces the room. He looks round.*

Interior. Room. Night.
LAW *and* JANE *in a corner, looking up at the window, blinking.*

Interior. Room. Day.
STOTT *at the window, closing the curtains. He turns into the room. The room is unrecognizable. The walls are hung with tapestries, an oval Florentine mirror, an oblong Italian Master. The floor is marble tiles. There are marble pillars with hanging plants, carved golden chairs, a rich carpet along the room's centre.*
STOTT *sits in a chair.* JANE *comes forward with a bowl of fruit.*
STOTT *chooses a grape. In the background* LAW, *in a corner, playing the flute.* STOTT *bites into the grape, tosses the bowl of fruit across the room. The fruit scatters.* JANE *rushes to collect it.*
STOTT *picks up a tray containing large marbles.*
He rolls the tray. The marbles knock against each other.
He selects a marble. He looks across the room at LAW *playing the flute.*

LAW *with flute.*
At the other end of the room STOTT *prepares to bowl.*
STOTT. Play!

STOTT *bowls.*

The marble crashes into the wall behind LAW.

LAW *stands, takes guard with his flute.*

STOTT. Play!
    STOTT *bowls.*

The marble crashes into the window behind LAW.

LAW *takes guard.*
STOTT. Play!
    STOTT *bowls. The marble hits* LAW *on the knee.*

LAW *hops.*

LAW *takes guard.*

STOTT. Play!
    STOTT *bowls.*

LAW *brilliantly cuts marble straight into golden fish tank. The
tank smashes. Dozens of fish swim across the marble tiles.*

JANE, *in the corner, applauds.*

LAW *waves his flute in acknowledgement.*

STOTT. Play!
  STOTT *bowls.*

Marble crashes into LAW'S *forehead. He drops.*

Interior. Kitchen. Night.
JANE *in the kitchen, putting spoonfuls of instant coffee into two cups.*

Interior. Room. Night.
The room is completely bare.
Bare walls. Bare floorboards. No furniture. One hanging bulb.
STOTT *and* LAW *at opposite ends of the room.*
They face each other. They are barefooted. They each hold a broken milk bottle. They are crouched, still.

LAW'S *face, sweating.*

STOTT'S *face, sweating.*

LAW *from* STOTT'S *viewpoint.*

STOT *from* LAW'S *viewpoint.*

JANE *pouring sugar from a packet into the bowl.*

LAW *pointing his bottle before him, his arm taut.*

STOTT *pointing his bottle before him, his arm taut.*

JANE *pouring milk from a bottle into a jug.*

STOTT *slowly advancing along bare boards.*

LAW *slowly advancing.*

JANE *pouring a small measure of milk into the cups.*

LAW *and* STOTT *drawing closer.*

JANE *putting sugar into the cups.*

The broken milk bottles, in shaking hands, almost touching.

The broken milk bottles fencing, not touching.

JANE *stirring milk, sugar and coffee in the cups.*

The broken milk bottles, in a sudden thrust, smashing together.

Record turning on a turntable. Sudden music.
Debussy's 'Girl With The Flaxen Hair'.

Exterior. Front area. Night.
LAW *standing centre, looking at the basement door.*
JANE *crouched by the wall. Rainhat. Raincoat.* LAW *wearing* STOTT'S *raincoat.*

Interior. Room.
Furnished as at the beginning.
STOTT *sitting by the fire, reading. He is smiling at his book.*

Exterior. Front area.
LAW *still.*

Interior. Room.
STOTT *turns a page.*
Doorbell.
STOTT *looks up, puts his book down, stands, goes into the hall.*

Interior. Room.
The room still. The fire burning.

Interior. Hall.
STOTT *approaches the front door. He opens it.*
Silence.
He stares at LAW. *From his position in the doorway* STOTT
cannot see JANE.
STOTT (*with great pleasure*). Law!
LAW (*smiling*). Hullo, Charles.
STOTT. Good God. Come in!
    STOTT *laughs.*
Come in!
    LAW *enters.*
I can't believe it!

LANDSCAPE

Landscape was first presented on radio by the BBC on 25th April, 1968, with the following cast:

BETH   Peggy Ashcroft
DUFF   Eric Porter

Directed by Guy Vaesen

The play was first presented on the stage by the Royal Shakespeare Company at the Aldwych Theatre on 2nd July, 1969, with the following cast:

BETH   Peggy Ashcroft
DUFF   David Waller

Directed by Peter Hall

DUFF: a man in his early fifties.
BETH: a woman in her late forties.
The kitchen of a country house.
A long kitchen table.
BETH sits in an armchair, which stands away from the table, to its left.
DUFF sits in a chair at the right corner of the table. The background, of a sink, stove, etc., and a window, is dim. Evening.

NOTE:

DUFF *refers normally to* BETH, *but does not appear to hear her voice.*
BETH *never looks at* DUFF, *and does not appear to hear his voice.*
Both characters are relaxed, in no sense rigid.

LANDSCAPE

BETH

I would like to stand by the sea. It is there.

Pause

I have. Many times. It's something I cared for. I've done it.

Pause

I'll stand on the beach. On the beach. Well ... it was very
fresh. But it was hot, in the dunes. But it was so fresh, on the
shore. I loved it very much.

Pause

Lots of people ...

Pause

People move so easily. Men. Men move.

Pause

I walked from the dune to the shore. My man slept in the
dune. He turned over as I stood. His eyelids. Belly button.
Snoozing how lovely.

Pause

Would you like a baby? I said. Children? Babies? Of our
own? Would be nice.

Pause

Women turn, look at me.

Pause

Our own child? Would you like that?

Pause

Two women looked at me, turned and stared. No. I was walking, they were still. I turned.

Pause

Why do you look?

Pause

I didn't say that, I stared. Then I was looking at them.

Pause

I am beautiful.

Pause

I walked back over the sand. He had turned. Toes under sand, head buried in his arms.

DUFF

The dog's gone. I didn't tell you.

Pause

I had to shelter under a tree for twenty minutes yesterday. Because of the rain. I meant to tell you. With some youngsters. I didn't know them.

Pause

Then it eased. A downfall. I walked up as far as the pond. Then I felt a couple of big drops. Luckily I was only a few yards from the shelter. I sat down in there. I meant to tell you.

Pause

Do you remember the weather yesterday? That downfall.?

BETH

He felt my shadow. He looked up at me standing above him.

DUFF

I should have had some bread with me. I could have fed the birds.

BETH

Sand on his arms.

DUFF

They were hopping about. Making a racket.

BETH

I lay down by him, not touching.

DUFF

There wasn't anyone else in the shelter. There was a man and woman, under the trees, on the other side of the pond. I didn't feel like getting wet. I stayed where I was.

Pause

Yes, I've forgotten something. The dog was with me.

Pause

BETH

Did those women know me? I didn't remember their faces. I'd never seen their faces before. I'd never seen those women before. I'm certain of it. Why were they looking at me? There's nothing strange about me. There's nothing strange about the way I look. I look like anyone.

DUFF

The dog wouldn't have minded me feeding the birds. Anyway, as soon as we got in the shelter he fell asleep. But even if he'd been awake . . . . .

Pause

BETH

They all held my arm lightly, as I stepped out of the car, or out of the door, or down the steps. Without exception. If they touched the back of my neck, or my hand, it was done so lightly. Without exception. With one exception.

DUFF

Mind you, there was a lot of shit all over the place, all along the paths, by the pond. Dogshit, duckshit . . . all kinds of shit . . . all over the paths. The rain didn't clean it up. It made it even more treacherous.

Pause

The ducks were well away, right over on their island. But I wouldn't have fed them, anyway. I would have fed the sparrows.

BETH

I could stand now. I could be the same. I dress differently, but I am beautiful.

Silence

DUFF

You should have a walk with me one day down to the pond, bring some bread. There's nothing to stop you.

Pause

I sometimes run into one or two people I know. You might remember them.

Pause

BETH

When I watered the flowers he stood, watching me, and watched me arrange them. My gravity, he said. I was so grave, attending

to the flowers, I'm going to water and arrange the flowers, I
said. He followed me and watched, standing at a distance from
me. When the arrangement was done I stayed still. I heard
him moving. He didn't touch me. I listened. I looked at the
flowers, blue and white, in the bowl.

Pause

Then he touched me.

Pause

He touched the back of my neck. His fingers, lightly, touching,
lightly, touching, the back, of my neck.

DUFF

The funny thing was, when I looked, when the shower was
over, the man and woman under the trees on the other side of
the pond had gone. There wasn't a soul in the park.

BETH

I wore a white beach robe. Underneath I was naked.

Pause

There wasn't a soul on the beach. Very far away a man was
sitting, on a breakwater. But even so he was only a pinpoint,
in the sun. And even so I could only see him when I was
standing, or on my way from the shore to the dune. When I
lay down I could no longer see him, therefore he couldn't see
me.

Pause

I may have been mistaken. Perhaps the beach was empty.
Perhaps there was no-one there.

Pause

He couldn't see .. my man .. anyway. He never stood up.

Pause

Snoozing how lovely I said to him. But I wasn't a fool, on that occasion. I lay quiet, by his side.

Silence

DUFF

Anyway . . .

BETH

My skin . . .

DUFF

I'm sleeping all right these days.

BETH

Was stinging.

DUFF

Right through the night, every night.

BETH

I'd been in the sea.

DUFF

Maybe it's something to do with the fishing. Getting to learn more about fish.

BETH

Stinging in the sea by myself.

DUFF

They're very shy creatures. You've got to woo them. You must never get excited with them. Or flurried. Never.

BETH

I knew there must be a hotel near, where we could get some
tea.

Silence

DUFF

Anyway . . . luck was on my side for a change. By the time I
got out of the park the pubs were open.

Pause

So I thought I might as well pop in and have a pint. I wanted
to tell you. I met some nut in there. First of all I had a word
with the landlord. He knows me. Then this nut came in. He
ordered a pint and he made a criticism of the beer. I had no
patience with it.

BETH

But then I thought perhaps the hotel bar will be open. We'll
sit in the bar. He'll buy me a drink. What will I order? But
what will he order? What will he want? I shall hear him say
it. I shall hear his voice. He will ask me what I would like
first. Then he'll order the two drinks. I shall hear him do it.

DUFF

This beer is piss, he said. Undrinkable. There's nothing wrong
with the beer, I said. Yes there is, he said, I just told you what
was wrong with it. It's the best beer in the area, I said. No it
isn't, this chap said, it's piss. The landlord picked up the mug
and had a sip. Good beer, he said. Someone's made a mistake,
this fellow said, someone's used this pintpot instead of the
boghole.

Pause

The landlord threw a half a crown on the bar and told him to take it. The pint's only two and three, the man said, I owe you three pence, but I haven't got any change. Give the threepence to your son, the landlord said, with my compliments. I haven't got a son, the man said, I've never had any children. I bet you're not even married, the landlord said. This man said: I'm not married. No-one'll marry me.

Pause

Then the man asked the landlord and me if we would have a drink with him. The landlord said he'd have a pint. I didn't answer at first, but the man came over to me and said: Have one with *me*. Have one with *me*.

Pause

He put down a ten bob note and said he'd have a pint as well.

Silence

BETH

Suddenly I stood. I walked to the shore and into the water. I didn't swim. I don't swim. I let the water billow me. I rested in the water. The waves were very light, delicate. They touched the back of my neck.

Silence

DUFF

One day when the weather's good you could go out into the garden and sit down. You'd like that. The open air. I'm often out there. The dog liked it.

Pause

I've put in some flowers. You'd find it pleasant. Looking at the flowers. You could cut a few if you liked. Bring them in. No-one would see you. There's no-one there.

Pause

That's where we're lucky, in my opinion. To live in Mr Sykes'
house in peace, no-one to bother us. I've thought of inviting
one or two people I know from the village in here for a bit of
a drink once or twice but I decided against it. It's not necessary.

Pause

You know what you get quite a lot of out in the garden?
Butterflies.

BETH

I slipped out of my costume and put on my beachrobe. Underneath I was naked. There wasn't a soul on the beach. Except
for an elderly man, far away on a breakwater. I lay down
beside him and whispered. Would you like a baby? A child?
Of our own? Would be nice.

Pause

DUFF

What did you think of that downfall?

Pause

Of course the youngsters I met under the first tree, during the
first shower, they were larking about and laughing. I tried to
listen, to find out what they were laughing about, but I
couldn't work it out. They were whispering. I tried to listen,
to find out what the joke was.

Pause

Anyway I didn't find out.

Pause

I was thinking ... when you were young ... you didn't laugh much. You were ... grave.

Silence

BETH

That's why he'd picked such a desolate place. So that I could draw in peace. I had my sketch book with me. I took it out. I took my drawing pencil out. But there was nothing to draw. Only the beach, the sea.

Pause

Could have drawn him. He didn't want it. He laughed.

Pause

I laughed, with him.

Pause

I waited for him to laugh, then I would smile, turn away, he would touch my back, turn me, to him. My nose .. creased. I would laugh with him, a little.

Pause

He laughed. I'm sure of it. So I didn't draw him.

Silence

DUFF

You were a first-rate housekeeper when you were young. Weren't you? I was very proud. You never made a fuss, you never got into a state, you went about your work. He could rely on you. He did. He trusted you, to run his house, to keep the house up to the mark, no panic.

Pause

Do you remember when I took him on that trip to the north? That long trip. When we got back he thanked you for looking after the place so well, everything running like clockwork.

Pause

You'd missed me. When I came into this room you stopped still. I had to walk all the way over the floor towards you.

Pause

I touched you.

Pause

But I had something to say to you, didn't I? I waited, I didn't say it then, but I'd made up my mind to say it, I'd decided I would say it, and I did say it, the next morning. Didn't I?

Pause

I told you that I'd let you down. I'd been unfaithful to you.

Pause

You didn't cry. We had a few hours off. We walked up to the pond, with the dog. We stood under the trees for a bit. I didn't know why you'd brought that carrier bag with you. I asked you. I said what's in that bag? It turned out to be bread. You fed the ducks. Then we stood under the trees and looked across the pond.

Pause

When we got back into this room you put your hands on my face and you kissed me.

BETH

But I didn't really want a drink.

Pause

I drew a face in the sand, then a body. The body of a woman. Then the body of a man, close to her, not touching. But they didn't look like anything. They didn't look like human figures. The sand kept on slipping, mixing the contours. I crept close to him and put my head on his arm, and closed my eyes. All those darting red and black flecks, under my eyelid. I moved my cheek on his skin. And all those darting red and black flecks, moving about under my eyelid. I buried my face in his side and shut the light out.

Silence

DUFF

Mr Sykes took to us from the very first interview, didn't he?

Pause

He said I've got the feeling you'll make a very good team. Do you remember? And that's what we proved to be. No question. I could drive well, I could polish his shoes well, I earned my keep. Turn my hand to anything. He never lacked for anything, in the way of being looked after. Mind you, he was a gloomy bugger.

Pause

I was never sorry for him, at any time, for his lonely life.

Pause

That nice blue dress he chose for you, for the house, that was very nice of him. Of course it was in his own interests for you to look good about the house, for guests.

BETH

He moved in the sand and put his arm around me.

Silence

DUFF

Do you like me to talk to you?

Pause

Do you like me to tell you about all the things I've been doing?

Pause

About all the things I've been thinking?

Pause

Mmmnn?

Pause

I think you do.

BETH

And cuddled me.

Silence

DUFF

Of course it was in his own interests to see that you were attractively dressed about the house, to give a good impression to his guests.

BETH

I caught a bus to the crossroads and then walked down the lane by the old church. It was very quiet, except for birds. There was an old man fiddling about on the cricket pitch, bending. I stood out of the sun, under a tree.

Pause

I heard the car. He saw me and stopped me. I stayed still. Then the car moved again, came towards me slowly. I moved round the front of it, in the dust. I couldn't see him for the sun, but he was watching me. When I got to the door it was locked. I looked through at him. He leaned over and opened the door. I got in and sat beside him. He smiled at me. Then he reversed, all in one movement, very quickly, quite straight, up the lane to the crossroads, and we drove to the sea.

Pause

DUFF

We're the envy of a lot of people, you know, living in this house, having this house all to ourselves. It's too big for two people.

BETH

He said he knew a very desolate beach, that no-one else in the world knew, and that's where we are going.

DUFF

I was very gentle to you. I was kind to you, that day. I knew you'd had a shock, so I was gentle with you. I held your arm on the way back from the pond. You put your hands on my face and kissed me.

BETH

All the food I had in my bag I had cooked myself, or prepared myself. I had baked the bread myself.

DUFF

The girl herself I considered unimportant. I didn't think it necessary to go into details. I decided against it.

BETH

The windows were open but we kept the hood up.

Pause

DUFF

Mr Sykes gave a little dinner party that Friday. He complimented you on your cooking and the service.

Pause

Two women. That was all. Never seen them before. Probably his mother and sister.

Pause

They wanted coffee late. I was in bed. I fell asleep. I would have come down to the kitchen to give you a hand but I was too tired.

Pause

But I woke up when you got into bed. You were out on your feet. You were asleep as soon as you hit the pillow. Your body . . . just fell back.

BETH

He was right. It was desolate. There wasn't a soul on the beach.

Silence

DUFF

I had a look over the house the other day. I meant to tell you. The dust is bad. We'll have to polish it up.

Pause

We could go up to the drawing room, open the windows. I could wash the old decanters. We could have a drink up there one evening, if it's a pleasant evening.

Pause

I think there's moths. I moved the curtain and they flew out.

Pause

BETH

Of course when I'm older I won't be the same as I am, I won't be what I am, my skirts, my long legs, I'll be older, I won't be the same.

DUFF

At least now ... at least now, I can walk down to the pub in peace and up to the pond in peace, with no-one to nag the shit out of me.

Silence

BETH

All it is, you see ... I said ... is the lightness of your touch, the lightness of your look, my neck, your eyes, the silence, that is my meaning, the loveliness of my flowers, my hands touching my flowers, that is my meaning.

Pause

I've watched other people. I've seen them.

Pause

All the cars zooming by. Men with girls at their sides. Bouncing up and down. They're dolls. They squeak.

Pause

All the people were squeaking in the hotel bar. The girls had long hair. They were smiling.

DUFF

That's what matters, anyway. We're together. That's what matters.

Silence

BETH

But I was up early. There was still plenty to be done and
cleared up. I had put the plates in the sink to soak. They had
soaked overnight. They were easy to wash. The dog was
up. He followed me. Misty morning. Comes from the river.

DUFF

This fellow knew bugger all about beer. He didn't know I'd
been trained as a cellarman. That's why I could speak with
authority.

BETH

I opened the door and went out. There was no-one about.
The sun was shining. Wet, I mean wetness, all over the
ground.

DUFF

A cellarman is the man responsible. He's the earliest up in the
morning. Give the drayman a hand with the barrels. Down
the slide through the cellarflaps. Lower them by rope to the
racks. Rock them on the belly, put a rim up them, use balance
and leverage, hike them up onto the racks.

BETH

Still misty, but thinner, thinning.

DUFF

The bung is on the vertical, in the bunghole. Spile the bung.
Hammer the spile through the centre of the bung. That lets
the air through the bung, down the bunghole, lets the beer
breathe.

BETH

Wetness all over the air. Sunny. Trees like feathers.

DUFF

Then you hammer the tap in.

BETH

I wore my blue dress.

DUFF

Let it stand for three days. Keep wet sacks over the barrels. Hose the cellar floor daily. Hose the barrels daily.

BETH

It was a beautiful autumn morning.

DUFF

Run water through the pipes to the bar pumps daily.

BETH

I stood in the mist.

DUFF

Pull off. Pull off. Stop pulling just before you get to the dregs. The dregs'll give you the shits. You've got an ullage barrel. Feed the slops back to the ullage barrel, send them back to the brewery.

BETH

In the sun.

DUFF

Dip the barrels daily with a brass rod. Know your gallonage. Chalk it up. Then you're tidy. Then you never get caught short.

BETH

Then I went back to the kitchen and sat down.

Pause

DUFF

This chap in the pub said he was surprised to hear it. He said
he was surprised to hear about hosing the cellar floor. He said
he thought most cellars had a thermostatically controlled
cooling system. He said he thought keg beer was fed with
oxygen through a cylinder. I said I wasn't talking about keg
beer, I was talking about normal draught beer. He said he
thought they piped the beer from a tanker into metal con-
tainers. I said they may do, but he wasn't talking about the
quality of beer I was. He accepted that point.

Pause

BETH

The dog sat down by me. I stroked him. Through the window
I could see down into the valley. I saw children in the valley.
They were running through the grass. They ran up the hill.

Long Silence

DUFF

I never saw your face. You were standing by the windows.
One of those black nights. A downfall. All I could hear was the
rain on the glass, smacking on the glass. You knew I'd come
in but you didn't move. I stood close to you. What were you
looking at? It was black outside. I could just see your shape in
the window, your reflection. There must have been some kind
of light somewhere. Perhaps just your face reflected, lighter
than all the rest. I stood close to you. Perhaps you were just
thinking, in a dream. Without touching you, I could feel your
bottom.

Silence

BETH

I remembered always, in drawing, the basic principles of

shadow and light. Objects intercepting the light cast shadows. Shadow is deprivation of light. The shape of the shadow is determined by that of the object. But not always. Not always directly. Sometimes it is only indirectly affected by it. Sometimes the cause of the shadow cannot be found.

Pause

But I always bore in mind the basic principles of drawing.

Pause

So that I never lost track. Or heart.

Pause

DUFF

You used to wear a chain round your waist. On the chain you carried your keys, your thimble, your notebook, your pencil, your scissors.

Pause

You stood in the hall and banged the gong.

Pause

What the bloody hell are you doing banging that bloody gong?

Pause

It's bullshit. Standing in an empty hall banging a bloody gong. There's no one to listen. No one'll hear. There's not a soul in the house. Except me. There's nothing for lunch. There's nothing cooked. No stew. No pie. No greens. No joint. Fuck all.

Pause

BETH

So that I never lost track. Even though, even when, I asked

him to turn, to look at me, but he turned to look at me but I couldn't see his look.

Pause

I couldn't see whether he was looking at me.

Pause

Although he had turned. And appeared to be looking at me.

DUFF

I took the chain off and the thimble, the keys, the scissors slid off it and clattered down. I booted the gong down the hall. The dog came in. I thought you would come to me, I thought you would come into my arms and kiss me, even ... offer yourself to me. I would have had you in front of the dog, like a man, in the hall, on the stone, banging the gong, mind you don't get the scissors up your arse, or the thimble, don't worry, I'll throw them for the dog to chase, the thimble will keep the dog happy, he'll play with it with his paws, you'll plead with me like a woman, I'll bang the gong on the floor, if the sound is too flat, lacks resonance, I'll hang it back on its hook, bang you against it swinging, gonging, waking the place up, calling them all for dinner, lunch is up, bring out the bacon, bang your lovely head, mind the dog doesn't swallow the thimble, slam—

Silence

BETH

He lay above me and looked down at me. He supported my shoulder.

Pause

So tender his touch on my neck. So softly his kiss on my cheek.

Pause

My hand on his rib.

Pause

So sweetly the sand over me. Tiny the sand on my skin.

Pause

So silent the sky in my eyes. Gently the sound of the tide.

Pause

Oh my true love I said.

SILENCE

Silence was first presented by the Royal Shakespeare Company at the Aldwych Theatre on 2nd July, 1969, with the following cast:

ELLEN: a girl in her twenties	Frances Cuka
RUMSEY: a man of forty	Anthony Bate
BATES: a man in his middle thirties	Norman Rodway

Directed by Peter Hall

Three areas.
A chair in each area.

SILENCE

RUMSEY

I walk with my girl who wears a grey blouse when she walks
and grey shoes and walks with me readily wearing her clothes
considered for me. Her grey clothes.

She holds my arm.

On good evenings we walk through the hills to the top of the
hill past the dogs the clouds racing just before dark or as dark
is falling when the moon

When it's chilly I stop her and slip her raincoat over her
shoulders or rainy slip arms into the arms, she twisting her
arms. And talk to her and tell her everything.

She dresses for my eyes.

I tell her my thoughts. Now I am ready to walk, her arm in
me her hand in me.

I tell her my life's thoughts, clouds racing. She looks up at
me or listens looking down. She stops in midsentence, my
sentence, to look up at me. Sometimes her hand has slipped
from mine, her arm loosened, she walks slightly apart, dog
barks.

ELLEN

There are two. One who is with me sometimes, and another.
He listens to me. I tell him what I know. We walk by the dogs.

Sometimes the wind is so high he does not hear me. I lead him to a tree, clasp closely to him and whisper to him, wind going, dogs stop, and he hears me.

But the other hears me.

BATES

Caught a bus to the town. Crowds. Lights round the market, rain and stinking. Showed her the bumping lights. Took her down around the dumps. Black roads and girders. She clutching me. This way the way I bring you. Pubs throw the doors smack into the night. Cars barking and the lights. She with me, clutching.

Brought her into this place, my cousin runs it. Undressed her, placed my hand.

ELLEN

I go by myself with the milk to the top, the clouds racing, all the blue changes, I'm dizzy sometimes, meet with him under some place.

One time visited his house. He put a light on, it reflected the window, it reflected in the window.

RUMSEY

She walks from the door to the window to see the way she has come, to confirm that the house which grew nearer is the same one she stands in, that the path and the bushes are the same, that the gate is the same. When I stand beside her and smile at her, she looks at me and smiles.

BATES

How many times standing clenched in the pissing dark waiting?

The mud, the cows, the river.

You cross the field out of darkness. You arrive.

You stand breathing before me. You smile.

I put my hands on your shoulders and press. Press the smile off your face.

ELLEN

There are two. I turn to them and speak. I look them in their eyes. I kiss them there and say, I look away to smile, and touch them as I turn.

Silence

RUMSEY

I watch the clouds. Pleasant the ribs and tendons of cloud.

I've lost nothing.

Pleasant alone and watch the folding light. My animals are quiet. My heart never bangs. I read in the evenings. There is no-one to tell me what is expected or not expected of me. There is nothing required of me.

BATES

I'm at my last gasp with this unendurable racket. I kicked open the door and stood before them. Someone called me Grandad and told me to button it. It's they should button it. Were I young . . .

One of them told me I was lucky to be alive, that I would have to bear it in order to pay for being alive, in order to give thanks for being alive.

It's a question of sleep. I need something of it, or how can I remain alive, without any true rest, having no solace, no constant solace, not even any damn inconstant solace.

I am strong, but not as strong as the bastards in the other room, and their tittering bitches, and their music, and their love.

If I changed my life, perhaps, and lived deliberately at night, and slept in the day. But what exactly would I do? What can be meant by living in the dark?

ELLEN

Now and again I meet my drinking companion and have a drink with her. She is a friendly woman, quite elderly, quite friendly. But she knows little of me, she could never know much of me, not really, not now. She's funny. She starts talking sexily to me, in the corner, with our drinks. I laugh.

She asks me about my early life, when I was young, never departing from her chosen subject, but I have nothing to tell her about the sexual part of my youth. I'm old, I tell her, my youth was somewhere else, anyway I don't remember. She does the talking anyway.

I like to get back to my room. It has a pleasant view. I have one or two friends, ladies. They ask me where I come from. I say of course from the country. I don't see much of them.

I sometimes wonder if I think. I heard somewhere about how many thoughts go through the brain of a person. But I couldn't remember anything I'd actually thought, for some time.

It isn't something that anyone could ever tell me, could ever reassure me about, nobody could tell, from looking at me, what was happening.

But I'm still quite pretty really, quite nice eyes, nice skin.

BATES *moves to* ELLEN

              BATES

Will we meet to-night?

              ELLEN

I don't know.

Pause

              BATES

Come with me to-night.

              ELLEN

Where?

              BATES

Anywhere. For a walk.

Pause

              ELLEN

I don't want to walk.

              BATES

Why not?

Pause

              ELLEN

I want to go somewhere else.

Pause

BATES

Where?

ELLEN

I don't know.

Pause

BATES

What's wrong with a walk?

ELLEN

I don't want to walk.

Pause

BATES

What do you want to do?

ELLEN

I don't know.

Pause

BATES

Do you want to go anywhere else?

ELLEN

Yes.

BATES

Where?

ELLEN

I don't know.

Pause

BATES

Do you want me to buy you a drink?

ELLEN

No.

Pause

BATES

Come for a walk.

ELLEN

No.

Pause

BATES

All right. I'll take you on a bus to the town. I know a place.
My cousin runs it.

ELLEN

No.

Silence

RUMSEY

It is curiously hot. Sitting weather, I call it. The weather sits,
does not move. Unusual. I shall walk down to my horse and
see how my horse is. He'll come towards me.

Perhaps he doesn't need me. My visit, my care, will be like
any other visit, any other care. I can't believe it.

BATES

I walk in my mind. But can't get out of the walls, into a wind.

Meadows are walled, and lakes. The sky's a wall.

Once I had a little girl. I took it for walks. I held it by its hand. It looked up at me and said, I see something in a tree, a shape, a shadow. It is leaning down. It is looking at us.

Maybe it's a bird, I said, a big bird, resting. Birds grow tired, after they've flown over the country, up and down in the wind, looking down on all the sights, so sometimes, when they reach a tree, with good solid branches, they rest.

Silence

ELLEN
When I run . . . when I run . . . when I run . . . over the grass
. . .

RUMSEY
She floats . . . under me. Floating . . . under me.

ELLEN
I turn. I turn. I wheel. I glide. I wheel. In stunning light. The horizon moves from the sun. I am crushed by the light.

Silence

RUMSEY
Sometimes I see people. They walk towards me, no, not so, walk in my direction, but never reaching me, turning left, or disappearing, and then reappearing, to disappear into the wood.

So many ways to lose sight of them, then to recapture sight of them. They are sharp at first sight . . . then smudged . . . then lost . . . then glimpsed again . . . then gone.

BATES

Funny. Sometimes I press my hand on my forehead, calmingly, feel all the dust drain out, let it go, feel the grit slip away. Funny moment. That calm moment.

ELLEN *moves to* RUMSEY

ELLEN

It's changed. You've painted it. You've made shelves. Everything. It's beautiful.

RUMSEY

Can you remember . . . when you were here last?

ELLEN

Oh yes.

RUMSEY

You were a little girl.

ELLEN

I was.

Pause

RUMSEY

Can you cook now?

ELLEN

Shall I cook for you?

RUMSEY

Yes.

ELLEN

Next time I come. I will.

Pause

RUMSEY

Do you like music?

ELLEN

Yes.

RUMSEY

I'll play you music.

Pause

RUMSEY

Look at your reflection.

ELLEN

Where?

RUMSEY

In the window.

ELLEN

It's very dark outside.

RUMSEY

It's high up.

ELLEN

Does it get darker the higher you get?

RUMSEY

No.

Silence

ELLEN

Around me sits the night. Such a silence. I can hear myself. Cup my ear. My heart beats in my ear. Such a silence. Is it me? Am I silent or speaking? How can I know? Can I know such things? No-one has ever told me. I need to be told things. I seem to be old. Am I old now? No-one will tell me. I must find a person to tell me these things.

BATES

My landlady asks me in for a drink. Stupid conversation. What are you doing here? Why do you live alone? Where do you come from? What do you do with yourself? What kind of life have you had? You seem fit. A bit grumpy. You can smile, surely, at something? Surely you have smiled, at a thing in your life? At something? Has there been no pleasantness in your life? No kind of loveliness in your life? Are you nothing but a childish old man, suffocating himself?

I've had all that. I've got all that. I said.

ELLEN

He sat me on his knee, by the window, and asked if he could kiss my right cheek. I nodded he could. He did. Then he asked, if, having kissed my right, he could do the same with my left. I said yes. He did.

Silence

RUMSEY

She was looking down. I couldn't hear what she said.

BATES

I can't hear you. Yes you can, I said.

RUMSEY

What are you saying? Look at me, she said.

BATES

I didn't. I didn't hear you, she said. I didn't hear what you said.

RUMSEY

But I am looking at you. It's your head that's bent.

Silence

BATES

The little girl looked up at me. I said: at night horses are quite happy. They stand about, then after a bit of a time they go to sleep. In the morning they wake up, snort a bit, canter, sometimes, and eat. You've no cause to worry about them.

ELLEN *moves to* RUMSEY

RUMSEY

Find a young man.

ELLEN

There aren't any.

RUMSEY

Don't be stupid.

ELLEN

I don't like them.

RUMSEY

You're stupid.

ELLEN

I hate them.

Pause

RUMSEY

Find one.

Silence

BATES

For instance, I said, those shapes in the trees, you'll find they're just birds, resting after a long journey.

ELLEN

I go up with the milk. The sky hits me. I walk in this wind to collide with them waiting.

There are two. They halt to laugh and bellow in the yard. They dig and punch and cackle where they stand. They turn to move, look round at me to grin. I turn my eyes from one, and from the other to him.

Silence

BATES

From the young people's room – silence. Sleep? Tender love?

It's of no importance.

Silence

RUMSEY

I walk with my girl who wears—

BATES

Caught a bus to the town. Crowds. Lights round—

Silence

ELLEN

After my work each day I walk back through people but I don't notice them. I'm not in a dream or anything of that sort. On the contrary. I'm quite wide awake to the world around me. But not to the people. There must be something in them to notice, to pay attention to, something of interest in them. In fact I know there is. I'm certain of it. But I pass through them noticing nothing. It is only later, in my room, that I remember. Yes, I remember. But I'm never sure that what I remember is of to-day or of yesterday or of a long time ago.

And then often it is only half things I remember, half things, beginnings of things.

My drinking companion for the hundredth time asked me if I'd ever been married. This time I told her I had. Yes, I told her I had. Certainly. I can remember the wedding.

Silence

RUMSEY

On good evenings we walk through the hills to the top of the hill past the dogs the clouds racing

ELLEN

Sometimes the wind is so high he does not hear me.

BATES

Brought her into this place, my cousin runs it.

ELLEN

all the blue changes, I'm dizzy sometimes

Silence

RUMSEY

that the path and the bushes are the same, that the gate is the same

BATES

You cross the field out of darkness.
You arrive.

ELLEN

I turn to them and speak.

Silence

RUMSEY

and watch the folding light.

BATES

and their tittering bitches, and their music, and their love.

ELLEN

They ask me where I come from. I say of course from the country.

Silence

BATES

Come with me tonight.

ELLEN

Where?

BATES

Anywhere. For a walk.

Silence

RUMSEY

My visit, my care, will be like any other visit, any other care.

BATES

I see something in a tree, a shape, a shadow.

Silence

ELLEN

When I run ...

RUMSEY

Floating ... under me.

ELLEN

The horizon moves from the sun.

Silence

RUMSEY

They are sharp at first sight ... then smudged ... then lost ...
then glimpsed again ... then gone.

BATES

feel all the dust drain out, let it go,

feel the grit slip away.

ELLEN

I look them in their eyes.

Silence

RUMSEY

It's high up.

ELLEN

Does it get darker the higher you get?

RUMSEY

No.

Silence

ELLEN

Around me sits the night. Such a silence.

BATES

I've had all that. I've got all that. I said.

ELLEN

I nodded he could.

Silence

RUMSEY

She was looking down.

BATES

Yes you can, I said.

RUMSEY

What are you saying?

BATES

I didn't hear you, she said.

RUMSEY

But I am looking at you. It's your head that's bent.

Silence

BATES

In the morning they wake up, snort a bit, canter, sometimes, and eat.

Silence

ELLEN

There aren't any.

RUMSEY

Don't be stupid.

ELLEN

I don't like them.

RUMSEY

You're stupid.

Silence

BATES

For instance, I said, those shapes in the trees.

ELLEN

I walk in this wind to collide with them waiting.

Silence

BATES

Sleep? Tender love? It's of no importance.

ELLEN

I kiss them there and say

Silence

RUMSEY

I walk

Silence

BATES

Caught a bus

Silence

ELLEN

Certainly. I can remember the wedding.

Silence

RUMSEY

I walk with my girl who wears a grey blouse

BATES

Caught a bus to the town. Crowds. Lights round the market

Long silence

Fade lights

REVUE SKETCHES

Night
That's Your Trouble
That's All
Applicant
Interview
Dialogue for Three

Night was first presented by Alexander H. Cohen Ltd. in an entertainment entitled *Mixed Doubles* at the Comedy Theatre on 9th April, 1969, with the following cast:

MAN	Nigel Stock
WOMAN	Vivien Merchant

Directed by Alexander Doré

That's Your Trouble, That's All, Applicant, Interview and *Dialogue for Three* were first presented on BBC Radio on the Third Programme between February and March 1964.

NIGHT

A woman and a man in their forties.
They sit with coffee.

MAN

I'm talking about that time by the river.

WOMAN

What time?

MAN

The first time. On the bridge. Starting on the bridge.

Pause

WOMAN

I can't remember.

MAN

On the bridge. We stopped and looked down at the river. It was
night. There were lamps lit on the towpath. We were alone.
We looked up the river. I put my hand on the small of your
waist. Don't you remember? I put my hand under your coat.

Pause

WOMAN

Was it winter?

MAN

Of course it was winter. It was when we met. It was our first
walk. You must remember that.

WOMAN

I remember walking. I remember walking with you.

MAN

The first time? Our first walk?

WOMAN

Yes, of course I remember that.

Pause

We walked down a road into a field, through some railings.
We walked to a corner of the field and then we stood by the
railings.

MAN

No. It was on the bridge that we stopped.

Pause

WOMAN

That was someone else.

MAN

Rubbish.

WOMAN

That was another girl.

MAN

It was years ago. You've forgotten.

Pause

I remember the light on the water.

WOMAN

You took my face in your hands, standing by the railings. You
were very gentle, you were very caring. You cared. Your eyes
searched my face. I wondered who you were. I wondered what
you thought. I wondered what you would do.

MAN

You agree we met at a party. You agree with that?

WOMAN

What was that?

MAN

What?

WOMAN

I thought I heard a child crying.

MAN

There was no sound.

WOMAN

I thought it was a child, crying, waking up.

MAN

The house is silent.

Pause

It's very late. We're sitting here. We should be in bed. I have
to be up early. I have things to do. Why do you argue?

WOMAN

I don't. I'm not. I'm willing to go to bed. I have things to do.
I have to be up in the morning.

Pause

MAN

A man called Doughty gave the party. You knew him. I had
met him. I knew his wife. I met you there. You were standing
by the window. I smiled at you, and to my surprise you
smiled back. You liked me. I was amazed. You found me
attractive. Later you told me. You liked my eyes.

WOMAN

You liked mine.

Pause

WOMAN

You touched my hand. You asked me who I was, and what I was, and whether I was aware that you were touching my hand, that your fingers were touching mine, that your fingers were moving up and down between mine.

MAN

No. We stopped on a bridge. I stood behind you. I put my hand under your coat, onto your waist. You felt my hand on you.

Pause

WOMAN

We had been to a party. Given by the Doughtys. You had known his wife. She looked at you dearly, as if to say you were her dear. She seemed to love you. I didn't. I didn't know you. They had a lovely house. By a river. I went to collect my coat, leaving you waiting for me. You had offered to escort me. I thought you were quite courtly, quite courteous, pleasantly mannered, quite caring. I slipped my coat on and looked out of the window, knowing you were waiting. I looked down over the garden to the river, and saw the lamplight on the water. Then I joined you and we walked down the road through railings into a field, must have been some kind of park. Later we found your car. You drove me.

Pause

MAN

I touched your breasts.

WOMAN

Where?

MAN

On the bridge. I felt your breasts.

WOMAN

Really?

MAN

Standing behind you.

WOMAN

I wondered whether you would, whether you wanted to, whether you would.

MAN

Yes.

WOMAN

I wondered how you would go about it, whether you wanted to, sufficiently.

MAN

I put my hands under your sweater, I undid your brassière, I felt your breasts.

WOMAN

Another night perhaps. Another girl.

MAN

You don't remember my fingers on your skin?

WOMAN

Were they in your hands? My breasts? Fully in your hands?

MAN

You don't remember my hands on your skin?

Pause

WOMAN

Standing behind me?

MAN

Yes.

WOMAN

But my back was against railings. I felt the railings . .
behind me. You were facing me. I was looking into your eyes.
My coat was closed. It was cold.

MAN

I undid your coat.

WOMAN

It was very late. Chilly.

MAN

And then we left the bridge and we walked down the towpath
and we came to a rubbish dump.

WOMAN

And you had me and you told me you had fallen in love with
me, and you said you would take care of me always, and you
told me my voice and my eyes, my thighs, my breasts, were
incomparable, and that you would adore me always.

MAN

Yes I did.

WOMAN

And you do adore me always.

MAN

Yes I do.

WOMAN

And then we had children and we sat and talked and you remembered women on bridges and towpaths and rubbish dumps.

MAN

And you remembered your bottom against railings and men holding your hands and men looking into your eyes.

WOMAN

And talking to me softly.

MAN

And your soft voice. Talking to them softly at night.

WOMAN

And they said I will adore you always.

MAN

Saying I will adore you always.

THAT'S YOUR TROUBLE

Two men in a park. One on the grass, reading. The other making cricket strokes with umbrella.

1 A. (*stopping in mid-stroke*): Eh, look at that bloke, what's he got on his back, he's got a sandwich board on his back.

2 B.: What about it?

3 A.: He wants to take it off, he'll get a headache.

4 B.: Rubbish.

5 A.: What do you mean?

6 B.: He won't get a headache.

7 A.: I bet he will.

8 B.: The neck! It affects his neck! He'll get a neckache.

9 A.: The strain goes up.

10 B.: Have you ever carried a sandwich board?

11 A.: Never.

12 B.: Then how do you know which way the strain *goes*? (*Pause.*) It goes down! The strain goes down, it starts with the neck and it goes down. He'll get a neckache and a backache.

13 A.: He'll get a headache in the end.

14 B.: There's no end.

15 A.: That's where the brain is.

16 B.: That's where the *what* is?

17 A.: The brain.

18 B.: It's nothing to do with the brain.

19 A.: Oh, isn't it?

20 B.: It won't go anywhere *near* his brain.

21 A.: That's where you're wrong.

22 B.: I'm not wrong. I'm right. (*Pause.*) You happen to be talking to a man who knows what he's talking

about. (*Pause.*) His brain doesn't come into it. If you've got a strain, it goes down. It's not like heat.

23 A.: What do you mean?

24 B. (*ferociously*): If you've got a strain it goes down! Heat goes up! (*Pause.*)

25 A.: You mean sound.

26 B.: I what?

27 A.: Sound goes up.

28 B.: Sound goes anywhere it likes! It all depends where you happen to be standing, it's a matter of physics, that's something you're just completely ignorant of, but you just try carrying a sandwich board and you'll find out soon enough. First the neck, then the shoulders, then the back, then it worms into the buttocks, that's where it worms. The buttocks. Either the right or the left, it depends how you carry your weight. Then right down the thighs – a straight drop to his feet and he'll collapse.

29 A.: He hasn't collapsed yet.

30 B.: He will. Give him a chance. A headache! How can he get a headache? He hasn't got anything on his head! I'm the one who's got the headache. (*Pause.*) You just don't know how to listen to what other people tell you, that's your trouble.

31 A.: I know what my trouble is.

32 B.: You don't know what your trouble is, my friend. That's your trouble.

THAT'S ALL

MRS A.: I always put the kettle on about that time.

MRS B.: Yes. (*Pause.*)

MRS A.: Then she comes round.

MRS B.: Yes. (*Pause.*)

MRS A.: Only on Thursdays.

MRS B.: Yes. (*Pause.*)

MRS A.: On Wednesdays I used to put it on. When she used to come round. Then she changed it to Thursdays.

MRS B.: Oh yes.

MRS A.: After she moved. When she used to live round the corner, then she always came in on Wednesdays, but then when she moved she used to come down to the butcher's on Thursdays. She couldn't find a butcher up there.

MRS B.: No.

MRS A.: Anyway, she decided she'd stick to her own butcher. Well, I thought, if she can't find a butcher, that's the best thing.

MRS B.: Yes. (*Pause.*)

MRS A.: So she started to come down on Thursdays. I didn't know she was coming down on Thursdays until one day I met her in the butcher.

MRS B.: Oh yes.

MRS A.: It wasn't my day for the butcher, I don't go to the butcher on Thursdays.

MRS B.: No, I know. (*Pause.*)

MRS A.: I go on Friday.

MRS B.: Yes. (*Pause.*)

MRS A.: That's where I see you.

MRS B.: Yes. (*Pause.*)

MRS A.: You're always in there on Fridays.

MRS B.: Oh yes. (*Pause.*)

MRS A.: But I happened to go in for a bit of meat, it turned out to be a Thursday. I wasn't going in for my usual weekly on Friday. I just slipped in, the day before.

MRS B.: Yes.

MRS A.: That was the first time I found out she couldn't find a butcher up there, so she decided to come back here, once a week, to her own butcher.

MRS B.: Yes.

MRS A.: She came on Thursday so she'd be able to get meat for the weekend. Lasted her till Monday, then from Monday to Thursday they'd have fish. She can always buy cold meat, if they want a change.

MRS B.: Oh yes. (*Pause.*)

MRS A.: So I told her to come in when she came down after she'd been to the butcher's and I'd put a kettle on. So she did. (*Pause.*)

MRS B.: Yes. (*Pause.*)

MRS A.: It was funny because she always used to come in Wednesdays. (*Pause.*) Still, it made a break. (*Long pause.*)

MRS B.: She doesn't come in no more, does she? (*Pause.*)

MRS A.: She comes in. She doesn't come in so much, but she comes in. (*Pause.*)

MRS B.: I thought she didn't come in. (*Pause.*)

MRS A.: She comes in. (*Pause.*) She just doesn't come in so much. That's all.

APPLICANT

An office. LAMB, *a young man, eager, cheerful, enthusiastic, is striding nervously, alone. The door opens.* MISS PIFFS *comes in. She is the essence of efficiency.*

PIFFS: Ah, good morning.

LAMB: Oh, good morning, miss.

PIFFS: Are you Mr. Lamb?

LAMB: That's right.

PIFFS [*studying a sheet of paper*]: Yes. You're applying for this vacant post, aren't you?

LAMB: I am actually, yes.

PIFFS: Are you a physicist?

LAMB: Oh yes, indeed. It's my whole life.

PIFFS [*languidly*]: Good. Now our procedure is, that before we discuss the applicant's qualifications we like to subject him to a little test to determine his psychological suitability. You've no objection?

LAMB: Oh, good heavens, no.

PIFFS: Jolly good.

MISS PIFFS *has taken some objects out of a drawer and goes to* LAMB. *She places a chair for him.*

PIFFS: Please sit down. [*He sits.*] Can I fit these to your palms?

LAMB [*affably*]: What are they?

PIFFS: Electrodes.

LAMB: Oh yes, of course. Funny little things.

She attaches them to his palms.

PIFFS: Now the earphones.

She attaches earphones to his head.

LAMB: I say how amusing.
PIFFS: Now I plug in.

She plugs in to the wall.

LAMB [*a trifle nervously*]: Plug in, do you? Oh yes, of course.
Yes, you'd have to, wouldn't you?

MISS PIFFS *perches on a high stool and looks down on* LAMB.

This help to determine my . . . my suitability does it?
PIFFS: Unquestionably. Now relax. Just relax. Don't think
about a thing.
LAMB: No.
PIFFS: Relax completely. Rela-a-a-x. Quite relaxed?

LAMB *nods.* MISS PIFFS *presses a button on the side of her
stool. A piercing high pitched buzz-hum is heard.* LAMB *jolts
rigid. His hands go to his earphones. He is propelled from the
chair. He tries to crawl under the chair.* MISS PIFFS *watches,
impassive. The noise stops.* LAMB *peeps out from under the
chair, crawls out, stands, twitches, emits a short chuckle and
collapses in the chair.*

PIFFS: Would you say you were an excitable person?
LAMB: Not—not unduly, no. Of course, I—
PIFFS: Would you say you were a moody person?
LAMB: Moody? No, I wouldn't say I was moody—well,
sometimes occasionally I—
PIFFS: Do you ever get fits of depression?
LAMB: Well, I wouldn't call them depression exactly—
PIFFS: Do you often do things you regret in the morning?
LAMB: Regret? Things I regret? Well, it depends what you
mean by often, really—I mean when you say often—
PIFFS: Are you often puzzled by women?
LAMB: Women?
PIFFS: Men.

LAMB: Men? Well, I was just going to answer the question about women—

PIFFS: Do you often feel puzzled?

LAMB: Puzzled?

PIFFS: By women.

LAMB: Women?

PIFFS: Men.

LAMB: Oh, now just a minute, I . . . Look, do you want separate answers or a joint answer?

PIFFS: After your day's work do you ever feel tired? Edgy? Fretty? Irritable? At a loose end? Morose? Frustrated? Morbid? Unable to concentrate? Unable to sleep? Unable to eat? Unable to remain seated? Unable to remain upright? Lustful? Indolent? On heat? Randy? Full of desire? Full of energy? Full of dread? Drained? of energy, of dread? of desire?

Pause.

LAMB [*thinking*]: Well, it's difficult to say really . . .

PIFFS: Are you a good mixer?

LAMB: Well, you've touched on quite an interesting point there—

PIFFS: Do you suffer from eczema, listlessness, or falling coat?

LAMB: Er . . .

PIFFS: Are you virgo intacta?

LAMB: I beg your pardon?

PIFFS: Are you virgo intacta?

LAMB: Oh, I say, that's rather embarrassing. I mean—in front of a lady—

PIFFS: Are you virgo intacta?

LAMB: Yes, I am, actually. I'll make no secret of it.

PIFFS: Have you always been virgo intacta?

LAMB: Oh yes, always. Always.

PIFFS: From the word go?

LAMB: Go? Oh yes, from the word go.

PIFFS: Do women frighten you?

She presses a button on the other side of her stool. The stage is plunged into redness, which flashes on and off in time with her questions.

PIFFS [*building*]: Their clothes? Their shoes? Their voices? Their laughter? Their stares? Their way of walking? Their way of sitting? Their way of smiling? Their way of talking? Their mouths? Their hands? Their feet? Their shins? Their thighs? Their knees? Their eyes?
Their [*Drumbeat*]. Their [*Drumbeat*]. Their [*Cymbal bang*]. Their [*Trombone chord*]. Their [*Bass note*].

LAMB [*in a high voice*]. Well it depends what you mean really—

The light still flashes. She presses the other button and the piercing buzz-hum is heard again. LAMB'S *hands go to his earphones. He is propelled from the chair, falls, rolls, crawls, totters and collapses.*

Silence.

He lies face upwards. MISS PIFFS *looks at him then walks to* LAMB *and bends over him.*

PIFFS: Thank you very much, Mr. Lamb. We'll let you know.

INTERVIEW

INTERVIEWER: Well, Mr. Jakes, how would you say things are in the pornographic book trade?

JAKES: I make 200 a week.

INTERVIEWER: 200?

JAKES: Yes, I make round about 200 a week at it.

INTERVIEWER: I see. So how would you say things were in the pornographic book trade?

JAKES: Oh, only fair.

INTERVIEWER: Only fair?

JAKES: Fair to middling.

INTERVIEWER: Why would you say that, Mr. Jakes?

JAKES: Well, it's got a lot to do with Xmas, between you and me.

INTERVIEWER: Xmas?

JAKES: Yes, well what happens is, you see, is that the trade takes a bit of a bashing round about Xmas time. Takes a good few months to recover from Xmas time, the pornographic book trade does.

INTERVIEWER: Oh, I see.

JAKES: Yes, what's got something to do with it is, you see, that you don't get all that many people sending pornographic books for Xmas presents. I mean, you get a few, of course, but not all that many. No, we can't really say that people in our trade get much benefit from the Xmas spirit, if you know what I mean.

INTERVIEWER: Well, I'm sorry to hear that, Mr. Jakes.

JAKES: Well, there you are. We make the best of it. (*Pause.*) I mean I put a sprig of holly ... here and there ... I put holly up all over the shop, but it doesn't seem to make much difference. (*Pause.*)

INTERVIEWER: What sort of people do you get in your shop, Mr. Jakes?

JAKES: I beg your pardon?

INTERVIEWER: What sort of people do you get in your shop?

JAKES: I'd rather not answer that question, thanks.

INTERVIEWER: Why not?

JAKES: I should think the security police could tell you a thing or two about that.

INTERVIEWER: Security police?

JAKES: Yes. They've got their dossiers, don't you worry about that.

INTERVIEWER: But we have no security police in this country.

JAKES: Don't you? You'd be surprised. They know all about it, take it from me. I've seen their dossiers.

INTERVIEWER: You've seen their dossiers?

JAKES: Dossiers? I've looked at more of their dossiers than you've had nights off.

INTERVIEWER: I see. Well, perhaps we'd better pass on to another question.

JAKES: Dossiers? I've been there morning and afternoon checking over their dossiers, identifying my customers, identifying their photographs right into the middle of the night, right into the middle of their dossiers.

INTERVIEWER: I had no idea –

JAKES: We've got them all taped in the pornographic book trade, don't you worry about that.

INTERVIEWER: Yes, well –

JAKES: You've no need to become anxious about *that*.

INTERVIEWER: Mr. Jakes –

JAKES: Every single individual that passes through my door goes out.

INTERVIEWER: What?

JAKES: Every single dirty-minded individual that passes

through my door goes straight out again. As soon as he's chosen his fancy – out he goes.

INTERVIEWER: You don't . . . keep them in?

JAKES: Keep them in! Never! I wouldn't keep one of them in my own little pornographic bookshop, not me. Not that they haven't begged, mind you. Begged. They've gone down on their bended knees and begged me to allow them to stay the night in the backroom, in the punishment section. Not me. Not since I got the word.

INTERVIEWER: I think perhaps –

JAKES (*confidentially*): You don't think the security police are the only people who've got dossiers, do you?

INTERVIEWER: No, I'm sure –

JAKES: You don't think that, do you? Get out of it. I'm up half the night doing my dossiers! I've got one on every single member of my clientele. And the day's coming, my boy, I can tell you.

INTERVIEWER: Coming?

JAKES: We're going to hold a special exhibition, see? We'll have them all in there, white in the face, peeping, peering, sweating, showing me false credentials to get to the top shelf, and then at a given moment we lock the doors and turn the floodlights on. And then we'll have them all revealed for what they are.

INTERVIEWER: What . . . are they?

JAKES: They're all the same, every single one of them. COMMUNISTS.

DIALOGUE FOR THREE

1ST MAN: Did I ever tell you about the woman in the blue dress? I met her in Casablanca. She was a spy. A spy in a blue dress. That woman was an agent for another power. She was tattooed on her belly with a pelican. Her belly was covered with a pelican. She could make that pelican waddle across the room to you. On all fours, sideways, feet first, arseupwards, any way you like. Her control was superhuman. Only a woman could possess it. Under her blue dress she wore a shimmy. And under her shimmy she wore a pelican.

2ND MAN: The snow has turned to slush.

1ST MAN: The temperature must have dropped.

WOMAN: Sometimes I think I'm not feminine enough for you.

1ST MAN: You are.

WOMAN: Or do you think I should be more feminine?

1ST MAN: No.

WOMAN: Perhaps I should be more masculine.

1ST MAN: Certainly not.

WOMAN: You think I'm too feminine?

1ST MAN: No.

WOMAN: If I didn't love you so much it wouldn't matter. Do you remember the first time we met? On the beach? In the night? All those people? And the bonfire? And the waves? And the spray? And the mist? And the moon? Everyone dancing, somersaulting, laughing? And you – standing silent, staring at a sandcastle in your sheer white trunks. The moon was behind you, in front of you, all over you, suffusing you, consuming you, you were transparent, translucent, a beacon. I was struck dumb, dumbstruck. Water rose up my legs. I could not move. I was rigid. Immovable. Our eyes met. Love at first sight. I held your gaze. And in your eyes, bold and unashamed, was desire. Brutal, demanding desire. Bestial, ruthless, remorseless. I stood there magnetised, hypnotised. Transfixed. Motionless and still. A spider caught in a web.

IST MAN (*to* 2ND MAN): You know who you remind me of? You remind me of Whipper Wallace, back in the good old days. He used to knock about with a chap called House Peters. Boghouse Peters we used to call him. I remember one day Whipper and Boghouse – he had a scar on his left cheek, Boghouse, caught in some boghouse brawl, I suppose – well, anyway, there they were, the Whipper and Boghouse, rolling down by the banks of the Euphrates this night, when up came a policeman . . . . . . up came this policeman . . . . . . up came a policeman . . . . . . this policeman . . . . . . approached . . . . . . Boghouse . . . . . . and the Whipper . . . . . . were questioned . . . . . . this night . . . . . . the Euphrates . . . . . . a policeman . . . . .

TEA PARTY

(Short Story)

AUTHOR'S NOTE

I wrote this short story in 1963, and in 1964 was commissioned by the B.B.C. to write a play for the European Broadcasting Union. I decided to treat the same subject in play form. In my view, the story is the more successful.

H.P.

TEA PARTY

My eyes are worse.

My physician is an inch under six feet. There is a grey strip in his hair, one, no more. He has a brown stain on his left cheek. His lampshades are dark blue drums. Each has a golden rim. They are identical. There is a deep black burn in his Indian carpet. His staff is bespectacled, to a woman. Through the blinds I hear the birds of his garden. Sometimes his wife appears, in white.

He is clearly sceptical on the subject of my eyes. According to him my eyes are normal, perhaps even better than normal. He finds no evidence that my sight is growing worse.

My eyes are worse. It is not that I do not see. I do see.

My job goes well. My family and I remain close friends. My two sons are my closest friends. My wife is closer. I am close friends with all my family, including my mother and my father. Often we sit and listen to Bach. When I go to Scotland I take them with me. My wife's brother came once, and was useful on the trip.

I have my hobbies, one of which is using a hammer and nails, or a screwdriver and screws, or various saws, on wood, constructing things or making things useful, finding a use for an object which appears to have no value. But it is not so easy to do this when you see double, or when you are blinded by the object, or when you do not see at all, or when you are blinded by the object.

My wife is happy. I use my imagination in bed. We love with the light on. I watch her closely, she watches me. In the morning her eyes shine. I can see them shining through her spectacles.

All winter the skies were bright. Rain fell at night. In the morning the skies were bright. My backhand flip was my strongest weapon. Taking position to face my wife's brother, across the dear table, my bat lightly clasped, my wrist flexing, I waited to loosen my flip to his forehand, watch him (*shocked*) dart and be beaten, flounder and sulk. My forehand was not so powerful, so swift. Predictably, he attacked my forehand. There was a ringing sound in the room, a rubber sound in the walls. Predictably, he attacked my forehand. But once far to the right on my forehand, and my weight genuinely disposed, I could employ my backhand flip, unanswerable, watch him flounder, skid and be beaten. They were close games. But it is not now so easy when you see the pingpong ball double, or do not see it at all or when, hurtling towards you at speed, the ball blinds you.

I am pleased with my secretary. She knows the business well and loves it. She is trustworthy. She makes calls to Newcastle and Birmingham on my behalf and is never fobbed off. She is respected on the telephone. Her voice is persuasive. My partner and I agree that she is of inestimable value to us. My partner and my wife often discuss her when the three of us meet for coffee or drinks. Neither of them, when discussing Wendy, can speak highly enough of her.

On bright days, of which there are many, I pull the blinds in my office in order to dictate. Often I touch her swelling body. She reads back, flips the page. She makes a telephone call to Birmingham. Even were I, while she speaks (holding the receiver lightly, her other hand poised for notes), to touch her swelling body, her call would still be followed to its conclusion. It is she who bandages my eyes, while I touch her swelling body.

I do not remember being like my sons in any way when I was a boy. Their reserve is remarkable. They seem stirred by no passion. They sit silent. An odd mutter passes between them. I can't hear you, what are you saying, speak up, I say. My wife says the same. I can't hear you, what are you saying, speak up. They are of an age. They work well at school, it appears. But at pingpong both are duds. As a boy I was wide awake, of passionate interests, voluble, responsive, and my eyesight was excellent. They resemble me in no way. Their eyes are glazed and evasive behind their spectacles.

My brother in law was best man at our wedding. None of my friends were at that time in the country. My closest friend, who was the natural choice, was called away suddenly on business. To his great regret, he was therefore forced to opt out. He had prepared a superb speech in honour of the groom, to be delivered at the reception. My brother in law could not of course himself deliver it, since it referred to the longstanding friendship which existed between Atkins and myself, and my brother in law knew little of me. He was therefore confronted with a difficult problem. He solved it by making his sister his central point of reference. I still have the present he gave me, a carved pencil sharpener, from Bali.

The day I first interviewed Wendy she wore a tight tweed skirt. Her left thigh never ceased to caress her right, and vice versa. All this took place under her skirt. She seemed to me the perfect secretary. She listened to my counsel wide-eyed and attentive, her hands calmly clasped, trim, bulgy, plump, rosy, swelling. She was clearly the possessor of an active and inquiring intelligence. Three times she cleaned her spectacles with a silken kerchief.

After the wedding my brother in law asked my dear wife to remove her glasses. He peered deep into her eyes. You have

married a good man, he said. He will make you happy. As he
was doing nothing at the time I invited him to join me in the
business. Before long he became my partner, so keen was his
industry, so sharp his business acumen.

Wendy's commonsense, her clarity, her discretion, are of
inestimable value to our firm.

With my eye at the keyhole I hear goosing, the squeak of them.
The slit is black, only the sliding gussle on my drum, the hiss
and flap of their bliss. The room sits on my head, my skull
creased on the brass and loathsome handle I dare not twist, for
fear of seeing black screech and scrape of my secretary writhing
blind in my partner's paunch and jungle.

My wife reached down to me. Do you love me, she asked. I do
love you, I spat into her eyeball. I shall prove it yet, I shall
prove it yet, what proof yet, what proof remaining, what proof
not yet given. All proof. (For my part, I decided on a more
cunning, more allusive strategem.) Do you love me, was my
counter.

The pingpong table streaked with slime. My hands pant to gain
the ball. My sons watch. They cheer me on. They are loud in
their loyalty. I am moved. I fall back on strokes, on gambits,
long since gone, flip, cut, chop, shtip, bluff to my uttermost. I
play the ball by nose. The twins hail my efforts gustily. But
my brother in law is no chump. He slams again, he slams again,
deep to my forehand. I skid, flounder, stare sightless into the
crack of his bat.

Where are my hammers, my screws, my saws?

How are you? asked my partner. Bandage on straight? Knots
tight?

The door slammed. Where was I? In the office or at home? Had
someone come in as my partner went out? Had he gone out?
Was it silence I heard, this scuffle, creak, squeal, scrape, gurgle
and muff? Tea was being poured. Heavy thighs (Wendy's? my
wife's? both? apart? together?) trembled in stilletos. I sipped
the liquid. It was welcome. My physician greeted me warmly.
In a minute, old chap, we'll take off those bandages. Have a
rock cake. I declined. The birds are at the bird bath, called his
white wife. They all rushed to look. My sons sent something
flying. *Someone?* Surely not. I had never heard my sons in such
good form. They chattered, chuckled, discussed their work
eagerly with their uncle. My parents were silent. The room
seemed very small, smaller than I had remembered it. I knew
where everything was, every particular. But its smell had
altered. Perhaps because the room was overcrowded. My wife
broke gasping out of a fit of laughter, as she was wont to do in
the early days of our marriage. Why was she laughing? Had
someone told her a joke? Who? Her sons? Unlikely. My sons
were discussing their work with my physician and his wife. Be
with you in a minute, old chap, my physician called to me.
Meanwhile my partner had the two women half stripped on a
convenient rostrum. Whose body swelled most? I had forgotten. I picked up a pingpong ball. It was hard. I wondered how
far he had stripped the women. The top halves or the bottom
halves? Or perhaps he was now raising his spectacles to view
my wife's swelling buttocks, the swelling breasts of my secretary. How could I verify this? By movement, by touch. But
that was out of the question. And could such a sight possibly
take place under the eyes of my own children? Would they
continue to chat and chuckle, as they still did, with my
physician? Hardly. However, it was good to have the bandage
on straight and the knots tight.

OLD TIMES

Old Times was first presented by the Royal Shakespeare Company at the Aldwych Theatre, London, on 1 June 1971, with the following cast:

DEELEY	Colin Blakely
KATE	Dorothy Tutin
ANNA	Vivien Merchant

All in their early forties

Directed by Peter Hall

The play was produced for television by the BBC in October 1975 with the following cast:

DEELEY	Anna Cropper
KATE	Barry Foster
ANNA	Mary Miller

Directed by Christopher Morahan

It was produced at the Theatre Royal, Haymarket, London, in April 1985 with the following cast:

DEELEY	Michael Gambon
KATE	Nicola Pagett
ANNA	Liv Ullmann

Directed by David Jones

A converted farmhouse
A long window up centre. Bedroom door up left. Front door up right.
Spare modern furniture
Two sofas. An armchair.
Autumn: Night.

ACT ONE

Light dim. Three figures discerned.

DEELEY *slumped in armchair, still.*
KATE *curled on a sofa, still.*
ANNA *standing at the window, looking out.*

Silence

Lights up on DEELEY *and* KATE, *smoking cigarettes.*

ANNA'S *figure remains still in dim light at the window.*

KATE

(*Reflectively.*) Dark.

Pause

DEELEY

Fat or thin?

KATE

Fuller than me. I think.

Pause

DEELEY

She was then?

KATE

I think so.

DEELEY

She may not be now.

Pause

Was she your best friend?

KATE

Oh, what does that mean?

DEELEY

What?

KATE

The word friend . . . when you look back . . . all that time.

DEELEY

Can't you remember what you felt?

Pause

KATE

It is a very long time.

DEELEY

But you remember her. She remembers you. Or why would she be coming here tonight?

KATE

I suppose because she remembers me.

Pause

DEELEY

Did you *think* of her as your best friend?

KATE

She was my only friend.

DEELEY

Your best and only.

KATE

My one and only.

Pause

If you have only one of something you can't say it's the best of anything.

DEELEY

Because you have nothing to compare it with?

KATE

Mmnn.

Pause

DEELEY

(*Smiling.*) She was incomparable.

KATE

Oh, I'm sure she wasn't.

Pause

DEELEY

I didn't know you had so few friends.

KATE

I had none. None at all. Except her.

DEELEY

Why her?

KATE

I don't know.

Pause

She was a thief. She used to steal things.

DEELEY

Who from?

KATE

Me.

DEELEY

What things?

KATE

Bits and pieces. Underwear.

DEELEY *chuckles*.

DEELEY

Will you remind her?

KATE

Oh . . . I don't think so.

Pause

                    DEELEY
Is that what attracted you to her?

                    KATE
What?

                    DEELEY
The fact that she was a thief.

                    KATE
No.

Pause

                    DEELEY
Are you looking forward to seeing her?

                    KATE
No.

                    DEELEY
I am. I shall be very interested.

                    KATE
In what?

                    DEELEY
In you. I'll be watching you.

                    KATE
Me? Why?

DEELEY

To see if she's the same person.

KATE

You think you'll find that out through me?

DEELEY

Definitely.

Pause

KATE

I hardly remember her. I've almost totally forgotten her.

Pause

DEELEY

Any idea what she drinks?

KATE

None.

DEELEY

She may be a vegetarian.

KATE

Ask her.

DEELEY

It's too late. You've cooked your casserole.

Pause

Why isn't she married? I mean, why isn't she bringing her husband?

KATE

Ask her.

DEELEY

Do I have to ask her everything?

KATE

Do you want me to ask your questions for you?

DEELEY

No. Not at all.

Pause

KATE

Of course she's married.

DEELEY

How do you know?

KATE

Everyone's married.

DEELEY

Then why isn't she bringing her husband?

KATE

Isn't she?

Pause

DEELEY

Did she mention a husband in her letter?

KATE

No.

DEELEY

What do you think he'd be like? I mean, what sort of man would she have married? After all, she was your best – your only – friend. You must have some idea. What kind of man would he be?

KATE

I have no idea.

DEELEY

Haven't you any curiosity?

KATE

You forget. I know her.

DEELEY

You haven't seen her for twenty years.

KATE

You've never seen her. There's a difference.

Pause

DEELEY

At least the casserole is big enough for four.

KATE

You said she was a vegetarian.

Pause

DEELEY

Did *she* have many friends?

KATE

Oh . . . the normal amount, I suppose.

DEELEY

Normal? What's normal? You had none.

KATE

One.

DEELEY

Is that normal?

Pause

She . . . had quite a lot of friends, did she?

KATE

Hundreds.

DEELEY

You met them?

KATE

Not all, I think. But after all, we were living together. There were visitors, from time to time. I met them.

DEELEY

Her visitors?

KATE

What?

DEELEY

Her visitors. Her friends. You had no friends.

KATE

Her friends, yes.

DEELEY

You met them.

Pause

(*Abruptly.*) You lived together?

KATE

Mmmnn?

DEELEY

You lived together?

KATE

Of course.

DEELEY

I didn't know that.

KATE

Didn't you?

DEELEY

You never told me that. I thought you just knew each other.

KATE

We did.

DEELEY

But in fact you lived with each other.

KATE

Of course we did. How else would she steal my underwear from me? In the street?

Pause

DEELEY

I knew you had shared with someone at one time . . .

Pause

But I didn't know it was her.

KATE

Of course it was.

Pause

DEELEY

Anyway, none of this matters.

ANNA *turns from the window, speaking, and moves down to them, eventually sitting on the second sofa.*

ANNA

Queuing all night, the rain, do you remember? my goodness, the Albert Hall, Covent Garden, what did we eat? to look back, half the night, to do things we loved, we were young then of course, but what stamina, and to work in the morning, and to a concert, or the opera, or the ballet, that night, you haven't forgotten? and then riding on top of the bus down Kensington High Street, and the bus conductors, and then dashing for the matches for the gasfire and then I suppose scrambled eggs, or did we? who cooked? both giggling and chattering, both huddling to the heat, then bed and sleeping, and all the hustle and bustle in the morning, rushing for the bus again for work, lunchtimes in Green Park, exchanging all our news, with our very own sandwiches, innocent girls, innocent secretaries, and then the night to come, and goodness knows what excitement in store, I mean the sheer expectation of it all, the looking-for-wardness of it all, and so poor, but to be poor and young, and a girl, in London then . . . and the cafés we found, almost private ones, weren't they? where artists and writers and sometimes actors collected, and others with dancers, we sat hardly breath-ing with our coffee, heads bent, so as not to be seen, so as not to disturb, so as not to distract, and listened and listened to all those words, all those cafés and all those people, creative un-doubtedly, and does it still exist I wonder? do you know? can you tell me?

Slight pause

DEELEY

We rarely get to London.

KATE *stands, goes to a small table and pours coffee from a pot.*

KATE

Yes, I remember.

She adds milk and sugar to one cup and takes it to ANNA. *She takes a black coffee to* DEELEY *and then sits with her own.*

DEELEY

(*to* ANNA.) Do you drink brandy?

ANNA

I would love some brandy.

DEELEY *pours brandy for all and hands the glasses. He remains standing with his own.*

ANNA

Listen. What silence. Is it always as silent?

DEELEY

It's quite silent here, yes. Normally.

Pause

You can hear the sea sometimes if you listen very carefully.

ANNA

How wise you were to choose this part of the world, and how sensible and courageous of you both to stay permanently in such a silence.

DEELEY

My work takes me away quite often, of course. But Kate stays here.

ANNA

No one who lived here would want to go far. I would not want to go far, I would be afraid of going far, lest when I returned the house would be gone.

DEELEY

Lest?

ANNA

What?

DEELEY

The word lest. Haven't heard it for a long time.

Pause

KATE

Sometimes I walk to the sea. There aren't many people. It's a long beach.

Pause

ANNA

But I would miss London, nevertheless. But of course I was a girl in London. We were girls together.

DEELEY

I wish I had known you both then.

ANNA

Do you?

DEELEY

Yes.

DEELEY *pours more brandy for himself.*

ANNA

You have a wonderful casserole.

DEELEY

What?

ANNA

I mean wife. So sorry. A wonderful wife.

DEELEY

Ah.

ANNA

I was referring to the casserole. I was referring to your wife's cooking.

DEELEY

You're not a vegetarian, then?

ANNA

No. Oh no.

DEELEY

Yes, you need good food in the country, substantial food, to keep you going, all the air . . . you know.

Pause

KATE

Yes, I quite like those kind of things, doing it.

ANNA

What kind of things?

KATE

Oh, you know, that sort of thing.

Pause

DEELEY

Do you mean cooking?

KATE

All that thing.

ANNA

We weren't terribly elaborate in cooking, didn't have the time, but every so often dished up an incredibly enormous stew, guzzled the lot, and then more often than not sat up half the night reading Yeats.

Pause

(*To herself.*) Yes. Every so often. More often than not.

ANNA *stands, walks to the window.*

And the sky is so still.

Pause

Can you see that tiny ribbon of light? Is that the sea? Is that the horizon?

DEELEY

You live on a very different coast.

ANNA

Oh, very different. I live on a volcanic island.

DEELEY

I know it.

ANNA

Oh, do you?

DEELEY

I've been there.

Pause

ANNA

I'm so delighted to be here.

DEELEY

It's nice I know for Katey to see you. She hasn't many friends.

ANNA

She has you.

DEELEY

She hasn't made many friends, although there's been every opportunity for her to do so.

ANNA

Perhaps she has all she wants.

DEELEY

She lacks curiosity.

ANNA

Perhaps she's happy.

Pause

KATE

Are you talking about me?

DEELEY

Yes.

ANNA

She was always a dreamer.

DEELEY

She likes taking long walks. All that. You know. Raincoat on.
Off down the lane, hands deep in pockets. All that kind of
thing.

ANNA *turns to look at* KATE.

ANNA

Yes.

DEELEY

Sometimes I take her face in my hands and look at it.

ANNA

Really?

DEELEY

Yes, I look at it, holding it in my hands. Then I kind of let it
go, take my hands away, leave it floating.

KATE

My head is quite fixed. I have it on.

DEELEY

(*To* ANNA.) It just floats away.

ANNA

She was always a dreamer.

ANNA *sits.*

Sometimes, walking, in the park, I'd say to her, you're dreaming, you're dreaming, wake up, what are you dreaming? and

she'd look round at me, flicking her hair, and look at me as if I were part of her dream.

Pause

One day she said to me, I've slept through Friday. No you haven't, I said, what do you mean? I've slept right through Friday, she said. But today is Friday, I said, it's been Friday all day, it's now Friday night, you haven't slept through Friday. Yes I have, she said, I've slept right through it, today is Saturday.

DEELEY

You mean she literally didn't know what day it was?

ANNA

No.

KATE

Yes I did. It was Saturday.

Pause

DEELEY

What month are we in?

KATE

September.

Pause

DEELEY

We're forcing her to think. We must see you more often. You're a healthy influence.

ANNA

But she was always a charming companion.

DEELEY

Fun to live with?

ANNA

Delightful.

DEELEY

Lovely to look at, delightful to know.

ANNA

Ah, those songs. We used to play them, all of them, all the time, late at night, lying on the floor, lovely old things. Sometimes I'd look at her face, but she was quite unaware of my gaze.

DEELEY

Gaze?

ANNA

What?

DEELEY

The word gaze. Don't hear it very often.

ANNA

Yes, quite unaware of it. She was totally absorbed.

DEELEY

In Lovely to look at, delightful to know?

KATE

(*To* ANNA.) I don't know that song. Did we have it?

DEELEY

(*Singing, to* KATE.) You're lovely to look at, delightful to know . . .

ANNA

Oh we did. Yes, of course. We had them all.

DEELEY

(*Singing.*) Blue moon, I see you standing alone . . .

ANNA

(*Singing.*) The way you comb your hair . . .

DEELEY

(*Singing.*) Oh no they can't take that away from me . . .

ANNA

(*Singing.*) Oh but you're lovely, with your smile so warm . . .

DEELEY

(*Singing.*) I've got a woman crazy for me. She's funny that way.

Slight pause

ANNA

(*Singing.*) You are the promised kiss of springtime . . .

DEELEY

(*Singing.*) And someday I'll know that moment divine,
When all the things you are, are mine!

Slight pause

ANNA

(*Singing.*) I get no kick from champagne,
          Mere alcohol doesn't thrill me at all,
          So tell me why should it be true –

DEELEY

(*Singing.*) That I get a kick out of you?

Pause

ANNA

(*Singing.*) They asked me how I knew
          My true love was true,
          I of course replied,
          Something here inside
          Cannot be denied.

DEELEY

(*Singing.*) When a lovely flame dies . . .

ANNA

(*Singing.*) Smoke gets in your eyes.

Pause

DEELEY

(*Singing.*) The sigh of midnight trains in empty stations . . .

Pause

ANNA

(*Singing.*) The park at evening when the bell has sounded . . .

Pause

DEELEY

(*Singing.*) The smile of Garbo and the scent of roses . . .

ANNA

(*Singing.*) The waiters whistling as the last bar closes . . .

DEELEY

(*Singing.*) Oh, how the ghost of you clings . . .

Pause

They don't make them like that any more.

Silence

What happened to me was this. I popped into a fleapit to see
Odd Man Out. Some bloody awful summer afternoon, walking
in no direction. I remember thinking there was something
familiar about the neighbourhood and suddenly recalled that
it was in this very neighbourhood that my father bought me
my first tricycle, the only tricycle in fact I ever possessed. Anyway, there was the bicycle shop and there was this fleapit showing Odd Man Out and there were two usherettes standing in
the foyer and one of them was stroking her breasts and the
other one was saying 'dirty bitch' and the one stroking her
breasts was saying 'mmnnn' with a very sensual relish and
smiling at her fellow usherette, so I marched in on this ex-
cruciatingly hot summer afternoon in the middle of nowhere
and watched Odd Man Out and thought Robert Newton was
fantastic. And I still think he was fantastic. And I would
commit murder for him, even now. And there was only one
other person in the cinema, one other person in the whole of

the whole cinema, and there she is. And there she was, very
dim, very still, placed more or less I would say at the dead
centre of the auditorium. I was off centre and have remained
so. And I left when the film was over, noticing, even though
James Mason was dead, that the first usherette appeared to be
utterly exhausted, and I stood for a moment in the sun, thinking I suppose about something and then this girl came out and
I think looked about her and I said wasn't Robert Newton
fantastic, and she said something or other, Christ knows what,
but looked at me, and I thought Jesus this is it, I've made a
catch, this is a trueblue pickup, and when we had sat down in
the café with tea she looked into her cup and then up at me and
told me she thought Robert Newton was remarkable. So it was
Robert Newton who brought us together and it is only Robert
Newton who can tear us apart.

Pause

ANNA

F. J. McCormick was good too.

DEELEY

I know F. J. McCormick was good too. But he didn't bring us
together.

Pause

DEELEY

You've seen the film then?

ANNA

Yes.

DEELEY

When?

ANNA

Oh . . . long ago.

Pause

DEELEY

(*To* KATE.) Remember that film?

KATE

Oh yes. Very well.

Pause

DEELEY

I think I am right in saying the next time we met we held hands. I held her cool hand, as she walked by me, and I said something which made her smile, and she looked at me, didn't you, flicking her hair back, and I thought she was even more fantastic than Robert Newton.

Pause

And then at a slightly later stage our naked bodies met, hers cool, warm, highly agreeable, and I wondered what Robert Newton would think of this. What would he think of this I wondered as I touched her profoundly all over.
(*To* ANNA.) What do you think he'd think?

ANNA

I never met Robert Newton but I do know I know what you mean. There are some things one remembers even though they may never have happened. There are things I remember which may never have happened but as I recall them so they take place.

DEELEY

What?

ANNA

This man crying in our room. One'night late I returned and found him sobbing, his hand over his face, sitting in the armchair, all crumpled in the armchair and Katey sitting on the bed with a mug of coffee and no one spoke to me, no one spoke, no one looked up. There was nothing I could do. I undressed and switched out the light and got into my bed, the curtains were thin, the light from the street came in, Katey still, on her bed, the man sobbed, the light came in, it flicked the wall, there was a slight breeze, the curtains occasionally shook, there was nothing but sobbing, suddenly it stopped. The man came over to me, quickly, looked down at me, but I would have absolutely nothing to do with him, nothing.

Pause

No, no, I'm quite wrong . . . he didn't move quickly . . . that's quite wrong . . . he moved . . . very slowly, the light was bad, and stopped. He stood in the centre of the room. He looked at us both, at our beds. Then he turned towards me. He approached my bed. He bent down over me. But I would have nothing to do with him, absolutely nothing.

Pause

DEELEY

What kind of man was he?

ANNA

But after a while I heard him go out. I heard the front door close, and footsteps in the street, then silence, then the footsteps fade away, and then silence.

Pause

But then sometime later in the night I woke up and looked across the room to her bed and saw two shapes.

DEELEY

He'd come back!

ANNA

He was lying across her lap on her bed.

DEELEY

A man in the dark across my wife's lap?

Pause

ANNA

But then in the early morning . . . he had gone.

DEELEY

Thank Christ for that.

ANNA

It was as if he had never been.

DEELEY

Of course he'd been. He went twice and came once.

Pause

Well, what an exciting story that was.

Pause

What did he look like, this fellow?

ANNA
Oh, I never saw his face clearly. I don't know.

DEELEY
But was he – ?

KATE *stands. She goes to a small table, takes a cigarette from a box and lights it. She looks down at* ANNA.

KATE
You talk of me as if I were dead.

ANNA
No, no, you weren't dead, you were so lively, so animated, you used to laugh –

DEELEY
Of course you did. I made you smile myself, didn't I? walking along the street, holding hands. You smiled fit to bust.

ANNA
Yes, she could be so . . . animated.

DEELEY
Animated is no word for it. When she smiled . . . how can I describe it?

ANNA
Her eyes lit up.

DEELEY

I couldn't have put it better myself.

DEELEY *stands, goes to cigarette box, picks it up, smiles at* KATE. KATE *looks at him, watches him light a cigarette, takes the box from him, crosses to* ANNA, *offers her a cigarette.* ANNA *takes one.*

ANNA

You weren't dead. Ever. In any way.

KATE

I said you talk about me as if I *am* dead. Now.

ANNA

How can you say that? How can you say that, when I'm looking at you now, seeing you so shyly poised over me, looking down at me –

DEELEY

Stop that!

Pause

KATE *sits.*
DEELEY *pours a drink.*

DEELEY

Myself I was a student then, juggling with my future, wondering should I bejasus saddle myself with a slip of a girl not long out of her swaddling clothes whose only claim to virtue was silence but who lacked any sense of fixedness, any sense of decisiveness, but was compliant only to the shifting winds, with which she went, but not *the* winds, and certainly not my winds, such as they are, but I suppose winds that only she understood, and that of course with no understanding whatsoever, at least as I understand the word, at least that's the way I figured it. A classic female figure, I said to myself, or is it a classic female posture, one way or the other long outworn.

Pause

That's the position as I saw it then. I mean, that is my categorical pronouncement on the position as I saw it then. Twenty years ago.

Silence

ANNA

When I heard that Katey was married my heart leapt with joy.

DEELEY

How did the news reach you?

ANNA

From a friend.

Pause

Yes, it leapt with joy. Because you see I knew she never did things loosely or carelessly, recklessly. Some people throw a stone into a river to see if the water's too cold for jumping, others, a few others, will always wait for the ripples before they will jump.

DEELEY

Some people do *what*? (*To* KATE.) What did she say?

ANNA

And I knew that Katey would always wait not just for the first emergence of ripple but for the ripples to pervade and pervade

the surface, for of course as you know ripples on the surface
indicate a shimmering in depth down through every particle of
water down to the river bed, but even when she felt that
happen, when she was assured it was happening, she still
might not jump. But in this case she did jump and I knew
therefore she had fallen in love truly and was glad. And I
deduced it must also have happened to you.

DEELEY

You mean the ripples?

ANNA

If you like.

DEELEY

Do men ripple too?

ANNA

Some, I would say.

DEELEY

I see.

Pause

ANNA

And later when I found out the kind of man you were I was
doubly delighted because I knew Katey had always been
interested in the arts.

KATE

I was interested once in the arts, but I can't remember now
which ones they were.

ANNA

Don't tell me you've forgotten our days at the Tate? and how
we explored London and all the old churches and all the old
buildings, I mean those that were left from the bombing, in the
City and south of the river in Lambeth and Greenwich? Oh
my goodness. Oh yes. And the Sunday papers! I could never
get her away from the review pages. She ravished them, and
then insisted we visit that gallery, or this theatre, or that
chamber concert, but of course there was so much, so much to
see and to hear, in lovely London then, that sometimes we
missed things, or had no more money, and so missed some
things. For example, I remember one Sunday she said to me,
looking up from the paper, come quick, quick, come with me
quickly, and we seized our handbags and went, on a bus, to
some totally obscure, some totally unfamiliar district and,
almost alone, saw a wonderful film called Odd Man Out.

Silence

DEELEY

Yes, I do quite a bit of travelling in my job.

ANNA

Do you enjoy it?

DEELEY

Enormously. Enormously.

ANNA

Do you go far?

DEELEY

I travel the globe in my job.

ANNA

And poor Katey when you're away? What does she do?

ANNA *looks at* KATE.

KATE

Oh, I continue.

ANNA

Is he away for long periods?

KATE

I think, sometimes. Are you?

ANNA

You leave your wife for such long periods? How can you?

DEELEY

I have to do a lot of travelling in my job.

ANNA

(*To* KATE.) I think I must come and keep you company when he's away.

DEELEY

Won't your husband miss you?

ANNA

Of course. But he would understand.

DEELEY

Does he understand now?

ANNA

Of course.

DEELEY

We had a vegetarian dish prepared for him.

ANNA

He's not a vegetarian. In fact he's something of a gourmet. We live in a rather fine villa and have done so for many years. It's very high up, on the cliffs.

DEELEY

You eat well up there, eh?

ANNA

I would say so, yes.

DEELEY

Yes, I know Sicily slightly. Just slightly. Taormina. Do you live in Taormina?

ANNA

Just outside.

DEELEY

Just outside, yes. Very high up. Yes, I've probably caught a glimpse of your villa.

Pause

My work took me to Sicily. My work concerns itself with life all over, you see, in every part of the globe. With people all over the globe. I use the word globe because the word world possesses emotional political sociological and psychological pretensions and resonances which I prefer as a matter of choice to do without, or shall I say to steer clear of, or if you like to reject. How's the yacht?

ANNA

Oh, very well.

DEELEY

Captain steer a straight course?

ANNA

As straight as we wish, when we wish it.

DEELEY

Don't you find England damp, returning?

ANNA

Rather beguilingly so.

DEELEY

Rather beguilingly so? (*To himself.*) What the hell does she mean by that?

Pause

Well, any time your husband finds himself in this direction my little wife will be only too glad to put the old pot on the old gas stove and dish him up something luscious if not voluptuous. No trouble.

Pause

I suppose his business interests kept him from making the trip. What's his name? Gian Carlo or Per Paulo?

KATE

(*To* ANNA.) Do you have marble floors?

ANNA

Yes.

KATE

Do you walk in bare feet on them?

ANNA

Yes. But I wear sandals on the terrace, because it can be rather severe on the soles.

KATE

The sun, you mean? The heat.

ANNA

Yes.

DEELEY

I had a great crew in Sicily. A marvellous cameraman. Irving Shultz. Best in the business. We took a pretty austere look at the women in black. The little old women in black. I wrote the film and directed it. My name is Orson Welles.

KATE

(*To* ANNA.) Do you drink orange juice on your terrace in the morning, and bullshots at sunset, and look down at the sea?

ANNA

Sometimes, yes.

DEELEY

As a matter of fact I am at the top of my profession, as a matter of fact, and I have indeed been associated with substantial numbers of articulate and sensitive people, mainly prostitutes of all kinds.

KATE

(*To* ANNA.) And do you like the Sicilian people?

DEELEY

I've been there. There's nothing more to see, there's nothing more to investigate, nothing. There's nothing more in Sicily to investigate.

KATE

(*To* ANNA.) Do you like the Sicilian people?

ANNA *stares at her*.

Silence

ANNA

(*Quietly*.) Don't let's go out tonight, don't let's go anywhere tonight, let's stay in. I'll cook something, you can wash your hair, you can relax, we'll put on some records.

KATE

Oh, I don't know. We could go out.

ANNA

Why do you want to go out?

KATE

We could walk across the park.

ANNA

The park is dirty at night, all sorts of horrible people, men hiding behind trees and women with terrible voices, they scream at you as you go past, and people come out suddenly

from behind trees and bushes and there are shadows everywhere and there are policemen, and you'll have a horrible
walk, and you'll see all the traffic and the noise of the traffic and
you'll see all the hotels, and you know you hate looking
through all those swing doors, you hate it, to see all that, all
those people in the lights in the lobbies all talking and moving
. . . and all the chandeliers . . .

Pause

You'll only want to come home if you go out. You'll want to
run home . . . and into your room. . . .

Pause

KATE

What shall we do then?

ANNA

Stay in. Shall I read to you? Would you like that?

KATE

I don't know.

Pause

ANNA

Are you hungry?

KATE

No.

DEELEY

Hungry? After that casserole?

Pause

KATE

What shall I wear tomorrow? I can't make up my mind.

ANNA

Wear your green.

KATE

I haven't got the right top.

ANNA

You have. You have your turquoise blouse.

KATE

Do they go?

ANNA

Yes, they do go. Of course they go.

KATE

I'll try it.

Pause

ANNA

Would you like me to ask someone over?

KATE

Who?

ANNA

Charley . . . or Jake?

KATE

I don't like Jake.

ANNA

Well, Charley . . . or . . .

KATE

Who?

ANNA

McCabe.

Pause

KATE

I'll think about it in the bath.

ANNA

Shall I run your bath for you?

KATE

(*Standing.*) No. I'll run it myself tonight.

KATE *slowly walks to the bedroom door, goes out, closes it.*

DEELEY *stands looking at* ANNA.
ANNA *turns her head towards him.*

They look at each other.

FADE

ACT TWO

The bedroom.
A long window up centre. Door to bathroom up left. Door to
sitting-room up right.

Two divans. An armchair.

The divans and armchair are disposed in precisely the same rela-
tion to each other as the furniture in the first act, but in reversed
positions.

Lights dim. ANNA *discerned sitting on divan. Faint glow from*
glass panel in bathroom door.

Silence.

Lights up. The other door opens. DEELEY *comes in with tray.*

DEELEY *comes into the room, places the tray on a table.*

DEELEY
Here we are. Good and hot. Good and strong and hot. You
prefer it white with sugar, I believe?

ANNA
Please.

DEELEY

(*Pouring.*) Good and strong and hot with white and sugar.

He hands her the cup.

Like the room?

ANNA

Yes.

DEELEY

We sleep here. These are beds. The great thing about these beds is that they are susceptible to any amount of permutation. They can be separated as they are now. Or placed at right angles, or one can bisect the other, or you can sleep feet to feet, or head to head, or side by side. It's the castors that make all this possible.

He sits with coffee.

Yes, I remember you quite clearly from The Wayfarers.

ANNA

The what?

DEELEY

The Wayfarers Tavern, just off the Brompton Road.

ANNA

When was that?

DEELEY

Years ago.

ANNA

I don't think so.

DEELEY

Oh yes, it was you, no question. I never forget a face. You sat in the corner, quite often, sometimes alone, sometimes with others. And here you are, sitting in my house in the country. The same woman. Incredible. Fellow called Luke used to go in there. You knew him.

ANNA

Luke?

DEELEY

Big chap. Ginger hair. Ginger beard.

ANNA

I don't honestly think so.

DEELEY

Yes, a whole crowd of them, poets, stunt men, jockeys, stand-up comedians, that kind of setup. You used to wear a scarf, that's right, a black scarf, and a black sweater, and a skirt.

ANNA

Me?

DEELEY

And black stockings. Don't tell me you've forgotten The Way-farers Tavern? You might have forgotten the name but you must remember the pub. You were the darling of the saloon bar.

ANNA

I wasn't rich, you know. I didn't have money for alcohol.

DEELEY

You had escorts. You didn't have to pay. You were looked after.
I bought you a few drinks myself.

ANNA

You?

DEELEY

Sure.

ANNA

Never.

DEELEY

It's the truth. I remember clearly.

Pause

ANNA

You?

DEELEY

I've bought you drinks.

Pause

Twenty years ago . . . or so.

ANNA

You're saying we've met before?

DEELEY

Of course we've met before.

Pause

We've talked before. In that pub, for example. In the corner. Luke didn't like it much but we ignored him. Later we all went to a party. Someone's flat, somewhere in Westbourne Grove. You sat on a very low sofa, I sat opposite and looked up your skirt. Your black stockings were very black because your thighs were so white. That's something that's all over now, of course, isn't it, nothing like the same palpable profit in it now, it's all over. But it was worthwhile then. It was worthwhile that night. I simply sat sipping my light ale and gazed . . . gazed up your skirt. You didn't object, you found my gaze perfectly acceptable.

ANNA

I was aware of your gaze, was I?

DEELEY

There was a great argument going on, about China or something, or death, or China *and* death, I can't remember which, but nobody but I had a thigh-kissing view, nobody but you had the thighs which kissed. And here you are. Same woman. Same thighs.

Pause

Yes. Then a friend of yours came in, a girl, a girl friend. She sat on the sofa with you, you both chatted and chuckled, sitting together, and I settled lower to gaze at you both, at both your thighs, squealing and hissing, you aware, she unaware, but then a great multitude of men surrounded me, and demanded my opinion about death, or about China, or whatever it was, and they would not let me be but bent down over me, so that what with their stinking breath and their broken teeth and the hair in their noses and China and death and their arses on the arms of my chair I was forced to get up and plunge my way through them, followed by them with ferocity, as if I were the cause of their argument, looking back through smoke, rushing to the table with the linoleum cover to look for one more full bottle of light ale, looking back through smoke, glimpsing two girls on the sofa, one of them you, heads close, whispering, no longer able to see anything, no longer able to see stocking or thigh, and then you were gone. I wandered over to the sofa. There was no one on it. I gazed at the indentations of four buttocks. Two of which were yours.

Pause

ANNA

I've rarely heard a sadder story.

DEELEY

I agree.

ANNA

I'm terribly sorry.

DEELEY

That's all right.

Pause

I never saw you again. You disappeared from the area. Perhaps you moved out.

ANNA

No. I didn't.

DEELEY

I never saw you in The Wayfarers Tavern again. Where were you?

ANNA

Oh, at concerts, I should think, or the ballet.

Silence

Katey's taking a long time over her bath.

DEELEY

Well, you know what she's like when she gets in the bath.

ANNA

Yes.

DEELEY

Enjoys it. Takes a long time over it.

ANNA

She does, yes.

DEELEY

A hell of a long time. Luxuriates in it. Gives herself a great soaping all over.

Pause

Really soaps herself all over, and then washes the soap off, sud by sud. Meticulously. She's both thorough and, I must say it, sensuous. Gives herself a comprehensive going over, and apart from everything else she does emerge as clean as a new pin. Don't you think?

ANNA

Very clean.

DEELEY

Truly so. Not a speck. Not a tidemark. Shiny as a balloon.

ANNA

Yes, a kind of floating.

DEELEY

What?

ANNA

She floats from the bath. Like a dream. Unaware of anyone standing, with her towel, waiting for her, waiting to wrap it round her. Quite absorbed.

Pause

Until the towel is placed on her shoulders.

Pause

DEELEY

Of course she's so totally incompetent at drying herself properly, did you find that? She gives herself a really good *scrub*, but can she with the same efficiency give herself an equally good *rub*? I have found, in my experience of her, that this is not in fact the case. You'll always find a few odd unexpected unwanted cheeky globules dripping about.

ANNA

Why don't you dry her yourself?

DEELEY

Would you recommend that?

ANNA

You'd do it properly.

DEELEY

In her bath towel?

ANNA

How out?

DEELEY

How out?

ANNA

How could you dry her out? Out of her bath towel?

DEELEY

I don't know.

ANNA

Well, dry her yourself, in her bath towel.

Pause

DEELEY

Why don't *you* dry her in her bath towel?

ANNA

Me?

DEELEY

You'd do it properly.

ANNA

No, no.

DEELEY

Surely? I mean, you're a woman, you know how and where and in what density moisture collects on women's bodies.

ANNA

No two women are the same.

DEELEY

Well, that's true enough.

Pause

I've got a brilliant idea. Why don't we do it with powder?

ANNA

Is that a brilliant idea?

DEELEY

Isn't it?

ANNA

It's quite common to powder yourself after a bath.

DEELEY

It's quite common to powder yourself after a bath but it's quite uncommon to be powdered. Or is it? It's not common where I come from, I can tell you. My mother would have a fit.

Pause

Listen. I'll tell you what. I'll do it. I'll do the whole lot. The towel and the powder. After all, I am her husband. But you can supervise the whole thing. And give me some hot tips while you're at it. That'll kill two birds with one stone.

Pause

(*To himself.*) Christ.

He looks at her slowly.

You must be about forty, I should think, by now.

Pause

If I walked into The Wayfarers Tavern now, and saw you sitting in the corner, I wouldn't recognize you.

The bathroom door opens. KATE *comes into the bedroom. She wears a bathrobe.*

She smiles at DEELEY *and* ANNA.

KATE
(*With pleasure.*) Aaahh.

She walks to the window and looks out into the night. DEELEY *and* ANNA *watch her.*

DEELEY *begins to sing softly.*

DEELEY
(*Singing.*) The way you wear your hat . . .

ANNA
(*Singing, softly.*) The way you sip your tea . . .

DEELEY
(*Singing.*) The memory of all that . . .

ANNA
(*Singing.*) No, no, they can't take that away from me . . .

KATE *turns from the window to look at them.*

ANNA
(*Singing.*) The way your smile just beams . . .

DEELEY
(*Singing.*) The way you sing off key . . .

ANNA
(*Singing.*) The way you haunt my dreams . . .

DEELEY
(*Singing.*) No, no, they can't take that away from me . . .

KATE *walks down towards them and stands, smiling.* ANNA *and*
DEELEY *sing again, faster on cue, and more perfunctorily.*

ANNA
(*Singing.*) The way you hold your knife –

DEELEY
(*Singing.*) The way we danced till three –

ANNA
(*Singing.*) The way you've changed my life –

DEELEY
No, no, they can't take that away from me.

KATE *sits on a divan.*

ANNA

(*To* DEELEY.) Doesn't she look beautiful?

DEELEY

Doesn't she?

KATE

Thank you. I feel fresh. The water's very soft here. Much softer than London. I always find the water very hard in London. That's one reason I like living in the country. Everything's softer. The water, the light, the shapes, the sounds. There aren't such edges here. And living close to the sea too. You can't say where it begins or ends. That appeals to me. I don't care for harsh lines. I deplore that kind of urgency. I'd like to go to the East, or somewhere like that, somewhere very hot, where you can lie under a mosquito net and breathe quite slowly. You know . . . somewhere where you can look through the flap of a tent and see sand, that kind of thing. The only nice thing about a big city is that when it rains it blurs everything, and it blurs the lights from the cars, doesn't it, and blurs your eyes, and you have rain on your lashes. That's the only nice thing about a big city.

ANNA

That's not the only nice thing. You can have a nice room and a nice gas fire and a warm dressing gown and a nice hot drink, all waiting for you for when you come in.

Pause

KATE

Is it raining?

ANNA

No.

KATE

Well, I've decided I will stay in tonight anyway.

ANNA

Oh good. I am glad. Now you can have a good strong cup of coffee after your bath.

ANNA *stands, goes to coffee, pours.*

I could do the hem on your black dress. I could finish it and you could try it on.

KATE

Mmmnn.

ANNA *hands her her coffee.*

ANNA

Or I could read to you.

DEELEY

Have you dried yourself properly, Kate?

KATE

I think so.

DEELEY

Are you sure? All over?

KATE

I think so. I feel quite dry.

DEELEY

Are you quite sure? I don't want you sitting here damply all over the place.

KATE *smiles*.

See that smile? That's the same smile she smiled when I was walking down the street with her, after Odd Man Out, well, quite some time after.
What did you think of it?

ANNA

It is a very beautiful smile.

DEELEY

Do it again.

KATE

I'm still smiling.

DEELEY

You're not. Not like you were a moment ago, not like you did then.

(*To* ANNA.) You know the smile I'm talking about?

KATE

This coffee's cold.

Pause

ANNA

Oh, I'm sorry. I'll make some fresh.

KATE

No, I don't want any, thank you.

Pause

Is Charley coming?

ANNA

I can ring him if you like.

KATE

What about McCabe?

ANNA

Do you really want to see anyone?

KATE

I don't think I like McCabe.

ANNA

Nor do I.

KATE

He's strange. He says some very strange things to me.

ANNA

What things?

KATE

Oh, all sorts of funny things.

ANNA

I've never liked him.

KATE

Duncan's nice though, isn't he?

ANNA

Oh yes.

KATE

I like his poetry so much.

Pause

But you know who I like best?

ANNA

Who?

KATE

Christy.

ANNA

He's lovely.

KATE

He's so gentle, isn't he? And his humour. Hasn't he got a lovely sense of humour? And I think he's . . . so sensitive. Why don't you ask him round?

DEELEY

He can't make it. He's out of town.

KATE

Oh, what a pity.

Silence

DEELEY

(*To* ANNA.) Are you intending to visit anyone else while you're in England? Relations? Cousins? Brothers?

ANNA

No. I know no one. Except Kate.

Pause

DEELEY

Do you find her changed?

ANNA

Oh, just a little, not very much. (*To* KATE.) You're still shy, aren't you?

KATE *stares at her.*

(*To* DEELEY.) But when I knew her first she was *so* shy, as shy as a fawn, she really was. When people leaned to speak to her she would fold away from them, so that though she was still standing within their reach she was no longer accessible to them. She folded herself from them, they were no longer able to speak or go through with their touch. I put it down to her upbringing, a parson's daughter, and indeed there was a good deal of Brontë about her.

DEELEY

Was she a parson's daughter?

ANNA

But if I thought Brontë I did not think she was Brontë in passion but only in secrecy, in being so stubbornly private.

Slight pause

I remember her first blush.

DEELEY

What? What was it? I mean why was it?

ANNA

I had borrowed some of her underwear, to go to a party. Later that night I confessed. It was naughty of me. She stared at me, nonplussed, perhaps, is the word. But I told her that in fact I had been punished for my sin, for a man at the party had spent the whole evening looking up my skirt.

Pause

DEELEY

She blushed at that?

ANNA

Deeply.

DEELEY

Looking up *your* skirt in *her* underwear. Mmnn.

ANNA

But from that night she insisted, from time to time, that I borrow her underwear – she had more of it than I, and a far greater range – and each time she proposed this she would blush, but propose it she did, nevertheless. And when there was anything to tell her, when I got back, anything of interest to tell her, I told her.

DEELEY

Did she blush then?

ANNA

I could never see then. I would come in late and find her reading under the lamp, and begin to tell her, but she would say no,

turn off the light, and I would tell her in the dark. She preferred to be told in the dark. But of course it was never completely dark, what with the light from the gasfire or the light
through the curtains, and what she didn't know was that,
knowing her preference, I would choose a position in the room
from which I could see her face, although she could not see
mine. She could hear my voice only. And so she listened and I
watched her listening.

DEELEY

Sounds a perfect marriage.

ANNA

We were great friends.

Pause

DEELEY

You say she was Brontë in secrecy but not in passion. What was
she in passion?

ANNA

I feel that is your province.

DEELEY

You feel it's my province? Well, you're damn right. It is my
province. I'm glad someone's showing a bit of taste at last. Of
course it's my bloody province. I'm her husband.

Pause

I mean I'd like to ask a question. Am I alone in beginning to
find all this distasteful?

ANNA

But what can you possibly find distasteful? I've flown from
Rome to see my oldest friend, after twenty years, and to meet
her husband. What is it that worries you?

DEELEY

What worries me is the thought of your husband rumbling
about alone in his enormous villa living hand to mouth on a
few hardboiled eggs and unable to speak a damn word of
English.

ANNA

I interpret, when necessary.

DEELEY

Yes, but you're here, with us. He's there, alone, lurching up
and down the terrace, waiting for a speedboat, waiting for a
speedboat to spill out beautiful people, at least. Beautiful
Mediterranean people. Waiting for all *that*, a kind of elegance
we know nothing about, a slim-bellied Cote d'Azur thing we
know absolutely nothing about, a lobster and lobster sauce
ideology we know fuck all about, the longest legs in the world,
the most phenomenally soft voices. I can hear them now. I
mean let's put it on the table, I have my eye on a number of
pulses, pulses all round the globe, deprivations and insults,
why should I waste valuable space listening to two –

KATE

(*Swiftly.*) If you don't like it go.

Pause

DEELEY

Go? Where can I go?

KATE

To China. Or Sicily.

DEELEY

I haven't got a speedboat. I haven't got a white dinner jacket.

KATE

China then.

DEELEY

You know what they'd do to me in China if they found me in a white dinner jacket. They'd bloodywell kill me. You know what they're like over there.

Slight pause

ANNA

You are welcome to come to Sicily at any time, both of you, and be my guests.

Silence

KATE *and* DEELEY *stare at her.*

ANNA

(*To* DEELEY, *quietly.*) I would like you to understand that I came here not to disrupt but to celebrate.

Pause

To celebrate a very old and treasured friendship, something that was forged between us long before you knew of our existence.

Pause

I found her. She grew to know wonderful people, through my introduction. I took her to cafés, almost private ones, where artists and writers and sometimes actors collected, and others with dancers, and we sat hardly breathing with our coffee, listening to the life around us. All I wanted for her was her happiness. That is all I want for her still.

Pause

DEELEY
(*To* KATE.) We've met before, you know. Anna and I.

KATE *looks at him.*

Yes, we met in the Wayfarers Tavern. In the corner. She took a fancy to me. Of course I was slimhipped in those days. Pretty nifty. A bit squinky, quite honestly. Curly hair. The lot. We had a scene together. She freaked out. She didn't have any bread, so I bought her a drink. She looked at me with big eyes, shy, all that bit. She was pretending to be you at the time. Did it pretty well. Wearing your underwear she was too, at the time. Amiably allowed me a gander. Trueblue generosity. Admirable in a woman. We went to a party. Given by philosophers. Not a bad bunch. Edgware road gang. Nice lot. Haven't seen any of them for years. Old friends. Always thinking. Spoke their thoughts. Those are the people I miss. They're all dead, anyway I've never seen them again. The Maida Vale group. Big Eric and little Tony. They lived somewhere near Paddington library. On the way to the party I took her into a café, bought her a cup of coffee, beards with faces. She thought she was you, said little, so little. Maybe she was you. Maybe it was you, having coffee with me, saying little, so little.

Pause

KATE

What do you think attracted her to you?

DEELEY

I don't know. What?

KATE

She found your face very sensitive, vulnerable.

DEELEY

Did she?

KATE

She wanted to comfort it, in the way only a woman can.

DEELEY

Did she?

KATE

Oh yes.

DEELEY

She wanted to comfort my face, in the way only a woman can?

KATE

She was prepared to extend herself to you.

DEELEY

I beg your pardon?

KATE

She fell in love with you.

DEELEY

With me?

KATE

You were so unlike the others. We knew men who were brutish, crass.

DEELEY

There really are such men, then? Crass men?

KATE

Quite crass.

DEELEY

But I was crass, wasn't I, looking up her skirt?

KATE

That's not crass.

DEELEY

If it was her skirt. If it was her.

ANNA

(*Coldly.*) Oh, it was my skirt. It was me. I remember your look
... very well. I remember you well.

KATE

(*To* ANNA.) But I remember you. I remember you dead.

Pause

I remember you lying dead. You didn't know I was watching you. I leaned over you. Your face was dirty. You lay dead, your

face scrawled with dirt, all kinds of earnest inscriptions, but
unblotted, so that they had run, all over your face, down to
your throat. Your sheets were immaculate. I was glad. I would
have been unhappy if your corpse had lain in an unwholesome
sheet. It would have been graceless. I mean as far as I was concerned. As far as my room was concerned. After all, you were
dead in my room. When you woke my eyes were above you,
staring down at you. You tried to do my little trick, one of my
tricks you had borrowed, my little slow smile, my little slow
shy smile, my bend of the head, my half closing of the eyes,
that we knew so well, but it didn't work, the grin only split the
dirt at the sides of your mouth and stuck. You stuck in your
grin. I looked for tears but could see none. Your pupils
weren't in your eyes. Your bones were breaking through your
face. But all was serene. There was no suffering. It had all
happened elsewhere. Last rites I did not feel necessary. Or any
celebration. I felt the time and season appropriate and that by
dying alone and dirty you had acted with proper decorum. It
was time for my bath. I had quite a lengthy bath, got out,
walked about the room, glistening, drew up a chair, sat naked
beside you and watched you.

Pause

When I brought him into the room your body of course had
gone. What a relief it was to have a different body in my room,
a male body behaving quite differently, doing all those things
they do and which they think are good, like sitting with one leg
over the arm of an armchair. We had a choice of two beds.
Your bed or my bed. To lie in, or on. To grind noses together,
in or on. He liked your bed, and thought he was different in it
because he was a man. But one night I said let me do something, a little thing, a little trick. He lay there in your bed. He

looked up at me with great expectation. He was gratified. He thought I had profited from his teaching. He thought I was going to be sexually forthcoming, that I was about to take a long promised initiative. I dug about in the windowbox, where you had planted our pretty pansies, scooped, filled the bowl, and plastered his face with dirt. He was bemused, aghast, resisted, resisted with force. He would not let me dirty his face, or smudge it, he wouldn't let me. He suggested a wedding instead, and a change of environment.

Slight pause

Neither mattered.

Pause

He asked me once, at about that time, who had slept in that bed before him. I told him no one. No one at all.

Long silence

ANNA *stands, walks towards the door, stops, her back to them.*

Silence

DEELEY *starts to sob, very quietly.*

ANNA *stands still.*

ANNA *turns, switches off the lamps, sits on her divan, and lies down.*

The sobbing stops

Silence

DEELEY *stands. He walks a few paces, looks at both divans.*

He goes to ANNA's *divan, looks down at her. She is still.*

Silence

DEELEY *moves towards the door, stops, his back to them.*

Silence

DEELEY *turns. He goes towards* KATE's *divan. He sits on her divan, lies across her lap.*

Long silence

DEELEY *very slowly sits up.*
He gets off the divan.
He walks slowly to the armchair.
He sits, slumped.

Silence

Lights up full sharply. Very bright.

DEELEY *in armchair.*
ANNA *lying on divan.*
KATE *sitting on divan.*

NO MAN'S LAND

No Man's Land was first presented by the National Theatre at the Old Vic, Waterloo, London, on 23rd April, 1975, with the following cast:

HIRST, *a man in his sixties*	Ralph Richardson
SPOONER, *a man in his sixties*	John Gielgud
FOSTER, *a man in his thirties*	Michael Feast
BRIGGS, *a man in his forties*	Terence Rigby

Designed by John Bury
Directed by Peter Hall

The play was subsequently presented at Wyndham's Theatre, London, from 15 July, 1975, with the same cast.

A large room in a house in North West London.
Well but sparely furnished. A strong and comfortable
straight-backed chair, in which HIRST sits.
A wall of bookshelves, with various items of pottery acting
as bookstands, including two large mugs.

Heavy curtains across the window.

The central feature of the room is an antique cabinet, with
marble top, brass gallery and open shelves, on which stands
a great variety of bottles: spirits, aperitifs, beers, etc.

ACT ONE

Summer.

Night.

SPOONER *stands in the centre of the room.*
He is dressed in a very old and shabby suit, dark faded shirt.
creased spotted tie.

HIRST *is pouring whisky at the cabinet.*
He is precisely dressed. Sports jacket. Well cut trousers.

HIRST

As it is?

SPOONER

As it is, yes please, absolutely as it is.

HIRST *brings him the glass.*

SPOONER

Thank you. How very kind of you. How very kind.

HIRST *pours himself a vodka.*

HIRST

Cheers.

SPOONER

Your health.

They drink. SPOONER *sips.* HIRST *drinks the vodka in one gulp.*
He refills his glass, moves to his chair and sits.
SPOONER *empties his glass.*

HIRST

Please help yourself.

SPOONER

Terribly kind of you.

SPOONER *goes to cabinet, pours. He turns.*

SPOONER

Your good health.

He drinks.

SPOONER

What was it I was saying, as we arrived at your door?

HIRST

Ah . . . let me see.

SPOONER

Yes! I was talking about strength. Do you recall?

HIRST

Strength. Yes.

SPOONER

Yes. I was about to say, you see, that there are some people who appear to be strong, whose idea of what strength consists of is persuasive, but who inhabit the idea and not the fact. What they possess is not strength but expertise. They have nurtured and maintain what is in fact a calculated posture. Half the time it works. It takes a man of intelligence and perception to stick a needle through that posture and discern the essential flabbiness of the stance. I am such a man.

HIRST

You mean one of the latter?

SPOONER

One of the latter, yes, a man of intelligence and perception. Not one of the former, oh no, not at all. By no means.

Pause

May I say how very kind it was of you to ask me in? In fact, you are kindness itself, probably always are kindness itself, now and in England and in Hampstead and for all eternity.

He looks about the room.

What a remarkably pleasant room. I feel at peace here. Safe from all danger. But please don't be alarmed. I shan't stay long. I never stay long, with others. They do not wish it. And that, for me, is a happy state of affairs. My only security, you see, my true comfort and solace, rests in the confirmation that I elicit from people of all kinds a common and constant level of indifference. It assures me that I am as I think myself to be, that I am fixed, concrete. To show interest in me or, good gracious, anything tending towards a positive liking of me, would cause in me a condition of the acutest alarm. Fortunately, the danger is remote.

Pause

I speak to you with this startling candour because you are clearly a reticent man, which appeals, and because you are a stranger to me, and because you are clearly kindness itself.

Pause

Do you often hang about Hampstead Heath?

HIRST

No.

SPOONER

But on your excursions . . however rare . . on your rare excursions . . you hardly expect to run into the likes of me? I take it?

HIRST

Hardly.

SPOONER

I often hang about Hampstead Heath myself, expecting nothing. I'm too old for any kind of expectation. Don't you agree?

HIRST

Yes.

SPOONER

A pitfall and snare, if ever there was one. But of course I observe a good deal, on my peeps through twigs. A wit once entitled me a betwixt twig peeper. A most clumsy construction, I thought.

HIRST

Infelicitous.

SPOONER

My Christ you're right.

Pause

HIRST

What a wit.

SPOONER

You're most acutely right. All we have left is the English language. Can it be salvaged? That is my question.

HIRST

You mean in what rests its salvation?

SPOONER

More or less.

HIRST

Its salvation must rest in you.

SPOONER

It's uncommonly kind of you to say so. In you too, perhaps, although I haven't sufficient evidence to go on, as yet.

Pause

HIRST

You mean because I've said little?

SPOONER

You're a quiet one. It's a great relief. Can you imagine two of us gabbling away like me? It would be intolerable.

Pause

By the way, with reference to peeping, I do feel it incumbent upon me to make one thing clear. I don't peep on sex. That's gone forever. You follow me? When my twigs happen to shall I say rest their peep on sexual conjugations, however periphrastic, I see only whites of eyes, so close, they glut me, no distance possible, and when you can't keep the proper distance between yourself and others, when you can no longer maintain an objective relation to matter, the game's not worth the candle, so forget it and remember that what is obligatory to keep in your vision is space, space in moonlight particularly, and lots of it.

HIRST

You speak with the weight of experience behind you.

SPOONER

And beneath me. Experience is a paltry thing. Everyone has it and will tell his tale of it. I leave experience to psychological interpreters, the wetdream world. I myself can do any graph of experience you wish, to suit your taste or mine. Child's play. The present will not be distorted. I am a poet. I am interested in where I am eternally present and active.

HIRST *stands, goes to cabinet, pours vodka.*

I have gone too far, you think?

HIRST

I'm expecting you to go very much further.

SPOONER

Really? That doesn't mean I interest you, I hope?

HIRST

Not in the least.

SPOONER

Thank goodness for that. For a moment my heart sank.

HIRST *draws the curtains aside, looks out briefly, lets curtain fall, remains standing.*

But nevertheless you're right. Your instinct is sound. I could go further, in more ways than one. I could advance, reserve my defences, throw on a substitute, call up the cavalry, or throw everything forward out of the knowledge that when joy overfloweth there can be no holding of joy. The point I'm trying to make, in case you've missed it, is that I am a free man.

HIRST *pours himself another vodka and drinks it. He puts the glass down, moves carefully to his chair, sits.*

HIRST

It's a long time since we had a free man in this house.

SPOONER

We?

HIRST

I.

SPOONER

Is there another?

HIRST

Another what?

SPOONER

People. Person.

HIRST

What other?

SPOONER

There are two mugs on that shelf.

HIRST

The second is for you.

SPOONER

And the first?

HIRST

Would you like to use it? Would you like some hot refreshment?

SPOONER

That would be dangerous. I'll stick to your scotch, if I may.

HIRST

Help yourself.

SPOONER

Thank you.

He goes to cabinet.

HIRST

I'll take a whisky with you, if you would be so kind.

SPOONER

With pleasure. Weren't you drinking vodka?

HIRST

I'll be happy to join you in a whisky.

SPOONER *pours.*

SPOONER

You'll take it as it is, as it comes?

HIRST

Oh, absolutely as it comes.

SPOONER *brings* HIRST *his glass.*

SPOONER

Your very good health.

HIRST

Yours.

They drink.

Tell me . . . do you often hang about Jack Straw's Castle?

SPOONER

I knew it as a boy.

HIRST

Do you find it as beguiling a public house now as it was in the days of the highwaymen, when it was frequented by highwaymen? Notably Jack Straw. The great Jack Straw. Do you find it much changed?

SPOONER

It changed my life.

HIRST

Good Lord. Did it really?

SPOONER

I refer to a midsummer night, when I shared a drink with a Hungarian émigré, lately retired from Paris.

HIRST

The same drink?

SPOONER

By no means. You've guessed, I would imagine, that he was an
erstwhile member of the Hungarian aristocracy?

HIRST

I did guess, yes.

SPOONER

On that summer evening, led by him, I first appreciated how
quiet life can be, in the midst of yahoos and hullabaloos. He
exerted on me a quite uniquely . . . calming influence, without
exertion, without any . . . desire to influence. He was so much
older than me. My expectations in those days, and I confess I
had expectations in those days, did not include him in their
frame of reference. I'd meandered over to Hampstead Heath,
a captive to memories of a more than usually pronounced
grisliness, and found myself, not much to my surprise, order-
ing a pint at the bar of Jack Straw's Castle. This achieved, and
having negotiated a path through a particularly repellent lick-
spittling herd of literati, I stumbled, unseeing, with my pint,
to his bald, tanned, unmoving table. How bald he was.

Pause

I think, after quite half my pint had descended, never to be
savoured again, that I spoke, suddenly, suddenly spoke, and
received . . . a response, no other word will do, a response, the
like of which –

HIRST

What was he drinking?

SPOONER

What?

HIRST

What was he drinking?

SPOONER

Pernod.

Pause

I was impressed, more or less at that point, by an intuition that he possessed a measure of serenity the like of which I had never encountered.

HIRST

What did he say?

SPOONER *stares at him.*

SPOONER

You expect me to remember what he said?

HIRST

No.

Pause

SPOONER

What he said . . . all those years ago . . . is neither here nor there. It was not what he said but possibly the way he sat which has remained with me all my life and has, I am quite sure, made me what I am.

Pause

And I met you at the same pub tonight, although at a different table.

Pause

And I wonder at you, now, as once I wondered at him. But will I wonder at you tomorrow, I wonder, as I still wonder at him today?

HIRST

I cannot say.

SPOONER

It cannot be said.

Pause

I'll ask you another question. Have you any idea from what I derive my strength?

HIRST

Strength? No.

SPOONER

I have never been loved. From this I derive my strength. Have you? Ever? Been loved?

HIRST

Oh, I don't suppose so.

SPOONER

I looked up once into my mother's face. What I saw there was nothing less than pure malevolence. I was fortunate to escape with my life. You will want to know what I had done to provoke such hatréd in my own mother.

HIRST

You'd pissed yourself.

SPOONER

Quite right. How old do you think I was at the time?

HIRST

Twenty eight.

SPOONER

Quite right. However, I left home soon after.

Pause

My mother remains, I have to say, a terribly attractive woman in many ways. Her buns are the best.

HIRST *looks at him.*

Her currant buns. The best.

HIRST

Would you be so kind as to pour me another drop of whisky?

SPOONER

Certainly.

SPOONER *takes the glass, pours whisky into it, gives it to* HIRST.

SPOONER

Perhaps it's about time I introduced myself. My name is Spooner.

HIRST

Ah.

SPOONER

I'm a staunch friend of the arts, particularly the art of poetry, and a guide to the young. I keep open house. Young poets

come to me. They read me their verses. I comment, give them
coffee, make no charge. Women are admitted, some of whom
are also poets. Some are not. Some of the men are not. Most of
the men are not. But with the windows open to the garden,
my wife pouring long glasses of squash, with ice, on a summer
evening, young voices occasionally lifted in unaccompanied
ballad, young bodies lying in the dying light, my wife moving
through the shadows in her long gown, what can ail? I mean
who can gainsay us? What quarrel can be found with what is,
au fond, a gesture towards the sustenance and preservation of
art, and through art to virtue?

HIRST

Through art to virtue. (*Raises glass.*) To your continued health.

SPOONER *sits, for the first time.*

SPOONER

When we had our cottage . . . when we had our cottage . . . we
gave our visitors tea, on the lawn.

HIRST

I did the same.

SPOONER

On the lawn?

HIRST

I did the same.

SPOONER

You had a cottage?

HIRST

Tea on the lawn.

SPOONER

What happened to them? What happened to our cottages? What happened to our lawns?

Pause

Be frank. Tell me. You've revealed something. You've made an unequivocal reference to your past. Don't go back on it. We share something. A memory of the bucolic life. We're both English.

Pause

HIRST

In the village church, the beams are hung with garlands, in honour of young women of the parish, reputed to have died virgin.

Pause

However, the garlands are not bestowed on maidens only, but on all who die unmarried, wearing the white flower of a blameless life.

Pause

SPOONER

You mean that not only young women of the parish but also young men of the parish are so honoured?

HIRST

I do.

SPOONER

And that old men of the parish who also died maiden are so garlanded?

HIRST

Certainly.

SPOONER

I am enraptured. Tell me more. Tell me more about the quaint little perversions of your life and times. Tell me more, with all the authority and brilliance you can muster, about the socio-politico-economic structure of the environment in which you attained to the age of reason. Tell me more.

Pause

HIRST

There is no more.

SPOONER

Tell me then about your wife.

HIRST

What wife?

SPOONER

How beautiful she was, how tender and how true. Tell me with what speed she swung in the air, with what velocity she came off the wicket, whether she was responsive to finger spin, whether you could bowl a shooter with her, or an offbreak with a legbreak action. In other words, did she google?

Silence

You will not say. I will tell you then . . . that my wife . . . had everything. Eyes, a mouth, hair, teeth, buttocks, breasts, absolutely everything. And legs.

HIRST

Which carried her away.

SPOONER

Carried who away? Yours or mine?

Pause

Is she here now, your wife? Cowering in a locked room, perhaps?

Pause

Was she ever here? Was she ever there, in your cottage? It is my duty to tell you you have failed to convince. I am an honest and intelligent man. You pay me less than my due. Are you, equally, being fair to the lady? I begin to wonder whether truly accurate and therefore essentially poetic definition means anything to you at all. I begin to wonder whether you do in fact truly remember her, whether you truly did love her, truly caressed her, truly did cradle her, truly did husband her, falsely dreamed or did truly adore her. I have seriously questioned these propositions and find them threadbare.

Silence

Her eyes, I take it, were hazel?

HIRST *stands, carefully. He moves, with a slight stagger, to the cabinet, pours whisky, drinks.*

HIRST

Hazel shit.

SPOONER

Good lord, good lord, do I detect a touch of the maudlin?

Pause

Hazel shit. I ask myself: Have I ever seen hazel shit? Or hazel eyes, for that matter?

HIRST *throws his glass at him, ineffectually. It bounces on the carpet.*

Do I detect a touch of the hostile? Do I detect – with respect – a touch of too many glasses of ale followed by the great malt which wounds? Which wounds?

Silence

HIRST

Tonight . . . my friend . . . you find me in the last lap of a race . . . I had long forgotten to run.

Pause

SPOONER

A metaphor. Things are looking up.

Pause

I would say, albeit on a brief acquaintance, that you lack the essential quality of manliness, which is to put your money

where your mouth is, to pick up a pintpot and know it to be a
pintpot, and knowing it to be a pintpot, to declare it as a pintpot, and to stay faithful to that pintpot as though you had given
birth to it out of your own arse. You lack that capability, in my
view.

Pause

Do forgive me my candour. It is not method but madness. So
you won't, I hope, object if I take out my prayer beads and
my prayer mat and salute what I take to be your impotence?

He stands.

I salute. And attend. And saluting and attending am at your
service all embracing. Heed me. I am a relevant witness. And
could be a friend.

HIRST *grips the cabinet, rigid.*

You need a friend, You have a long hike, my lad, up which,
presently, you slog unfriended. Let me perhaps be your boat-
man. For if and when we talk of a river we talk of a deep and
dank architecture. In other words, never disdain a helping
hand, especially one of such rare quality. And it is not only the
quality of my offer which is rare, it is the act itself, the offer
itself – quite without precedent. I offer myself to you as a
friend. Think before you speak.

HIRST *attempts to move, stops, grips the cabinet.*

Remember this. You've lost your wife of hazel hue, you've lost
her and what can you do, she will no more come back to you,
with a tillifola tillifola tillifoladi-foladi-foloo.

HIRST

No.

Pause

No man's land . . . does not move . . . or change . . . or grow
old . . . remains . . . forever . . . icy . . . silent.

HIRST *loosens his grip on the cabinet, staggers, across the room,
holds on to a chair.*

He waits, moves, falls.

He waits, gets to his feet, moves, falls.

SPOONER *watches.*

HIRST *crawls towards the door, manages to open it, crawls out of
the door.*

SPOONER *remains still.*

SPOONER

I have known this before. The exit through the door, by way of
belly and floor.

*He looks at the room, walks about it, looking at each object closely,
stops, hands behind his back, surveying the room.*

A door, somewhere in the house, closes.

Silence.

The front door opens, and slams sharply.

SPOONER *stiffens, is still.*

FOSTER *enters the room. He is casually dressed.*

He stops still upon seeing SPOONER. *He stands, looking at*
SPOONER.

Silence

FOSTER
What are you drinking? Christ I'm thirsty. How are you? I'm
parched.

He goes to cabinet, opens a bottle of beer, pours.

What are you drinking? It's bloody late. I'm worn to a frazzle.
This is what I want. (*He drinks.*) Taxi? No chance. Taxi
drivers are against me. Something about me. Some unknown
factor. My gait, perhaps. Or perhaps because I travel incog-
nito. Oh, that's better. Works wonders. How are you? What
are you drinking? Who are you? I thought I'd never make it.
What a hike. And not only that. I'm defenceless. I don't
carry a gun in London. But I'm not bothered. Once you've
done the East you've done it all. I've done the East. But I still
like a nice lighthouse like this one. Have you met your host?
He's my father. It was our night off tonight, you see. He was
going to stay at home, listen to some lieder. I hope he had a

quiet and pleasant evening. Who are you, by the way? What are you drinking?

SPOONER
I'm a friend of his.

FOSTER
You're not typical.

BRIGGS *comes into the room, stops. He is casually dressed, stocky.*

BRIGGS
Who's this?

FOSTER
His name's Friend. This is Mr. Briggs. Mr. Friend – Mr. Briggs. I'm Mr. Foster. Old English stock. John Foster. Jack. Jack Foster. Old English name. Foster. John Foster. Jack Foster. Foster. This man's name is Briggs.

Pause

BRIGGS
I've seen Mr. Friend before.

FOSTER
Seen him before?

BRIGGS
I know him.

FOSTER
Do you really?

BRIGGS
I've seen you before.

SPOONER

Possibly, possibly.

BRIGGS

Yes. You collect the beermugs from the tables in a pub in Chalk Farm.

SPOONER

The landlord's a friend of mine. When he's shorthanded, I give him a helping hand.

BRIGGS

Who says the landlord's a friend of yours?

FOSTER

He does.

BRIGGS

I'm talking about The Bull's Head in Chalk Farm.

SPOONER

Yes, yes. So am I.

BRIGGS

So am I.

FOSTER

I know The Bull's Head. The landlord's a friend of mine.

BRIGGS

He collects the mugs.

FOSTER

A firstclass pub. I've known the landlord for years.

BRIGGS

He says he's a friend of the landlord.

FOSTER

He says he's a friend of our friend too.

BRIGGS

What friend?

FOSTER

Our host.

BRIGGS

He's a bloody friend of everyone then.

FOSTER

He's everybody's bloody friend. How many friends have you got altogether, Mr. Friend?

BRIGGS

He probably couldn't count them.

FOSTER

Well, there's me too, now. I'm another one of your new friends. I'm your newest new friend. Not him. Not Briggs. He's nobody's fucking friend. People tend to be a little wary of Briggs. They balk at giving him their all. But me they like at first sight.

BRIGGS

Sometimes they love you at first sight.

FOSTER

Sometimes they do. That's why, when I travel, I get all the gold, nobody offers me dross. People take an immediate shine to me, especially women, especially in Siam or Bali. He knows I'm not a liar. Tell him about the Siamese girls.

BRIGGS

They loved him at first sight.

FOSTER

(*To* SPOONER.) You're not Siamese though, are you?

BRIGGS

He's a very long way from being Siamese.

FOSTER

Ever been out there?

SPOONER

I've been to Amsterdam.

FOSTER *and* BRIGGS *stare at him.*

I mean that was the last place . . . I visited. I know Europe well.
My name is Spooner, by the way. Yes, one afternoon in
Amsterdam . . . I was sitting outside a café by a canal. The
weather was superb. At another table, in shadow, was a man
whistling under his breath, sitting very still, almost rigid. At
the side of the canal was a fisherman. He caught a fish. He
lifted it high. The waiter cheered and applauded, the two men,
the waiter and the fisherman, laughed. A little girl, passing,
laughed. Two lovers, passing, kissed. The fish was lofted, on the
rod. The fish and the rod glinted in the sun, as they swayed.
The fisherman's cheeks were flushed, with pleasure. I decided
to paint a picture – of the canal, the waiter, the child, the
fisherman, the lovers, the fish, and in background, in shadow,
the man at the other table, and to call it The Whistler. The
Whistler. If you had seen the picture, and the title, would the
title have baffled you?

Pause

FOSTER

(*To* BRIGGS.) Do you want to answer that question?

BRIGGS

No. Go on. You answer it.

FOSTER

Well, speaking for myself, I think I would have been baffled by that title. But I might have appreciated the picture. I might even have been grateful for it.

Pause

Did you hear what I said? I might have been grateful for the picture. A good work of art tends to move me. You follow me? I'm not a cunt, you know.

Pause

I'm very interested to hear you're a painter. You do it in your spare time, I suppose?

SPOONER

Quite.

FOSTER

Did you ever paint that picture, The Whistler?

SPOONER

Not yet, I'm afraid.

FOSTER

Don't leave it too long. You might lose the inspiration.

BRIGGS

Ever painted a beermug?

SPOONER

You must come and see my collection, any time you wish.

BRIGGS

What of, beermugs?

SPOONER

No, no. Paintings.

FOSTER

Where do you keep it?

SPOONER

At my house in the country. You would receive the warmest of welcomes.

FOSTER

Who from?

SPOONER

My wife. My two daughters.

FOSTER

Really? Would they like me? What do you think? Would they love me at first sight?

SPOONER

(*Laughing.*) Quite possibly.

FOSTER

What about him?

SPOONER *looks at* BRIGGS.

SPOONER

They are remarkably gracious women.

FOSTER

You're a lucky man. What are you drinking?

SPOONER

Scotch.

FOSTER *goes to cabinet, pours scotch, stands holding glass.*

FOSTER

What do you make of this? When I was out East . . . once . . a kind of old stinking tramp, bollock naked, asked me for a few bob. I didn't know him. He was a complete stranger. But I could see immediately he wasn't a man to trust. He had a dog with him. They only had about one eye between them. So I threw him some sort of coin. He caught this bloody coin, looked at it with a bit of disaste, and then he threw the coin back. Well, automatically I went to catch it, I clutched at it, but the bloody coin disappeared into thin air. It didn't drop anywhere. It just disappeared . . into thin air . . on its way towards me. He then let out a few curses and pissed off, with his dog. Oh, here's your whisky, by the way. (*Hands it to him.*) What do you make of that incident?

SPOONER

He was a con artist.

FOSTER

Do you think so?

SPOONER

You would be wise to grant the event no integrity whatsoever.

FOSTER

You don't subscribe to the mystery of the Orient?

SPOONER

A typical Eastern contrick.

FOSTER

Double Dutch, you mean?

SPOONER

Certainly. Your good health. (*Drinks.*)

HIRST *enters, wearing a dressing-gown.*

BRIGGS *goes to cabinet, pours whisky.*

HIRST

I can't sleep. I slept briefly. I think. Perhaps it was sufficient.
Yes. I woke up, out of a dream. I feel cheerful. Who'll give me
a glass of whisky?

HIRST *sits.* BRIGGS *brings him whisky.*

My goodness, is this for me? How did you know? You knew.
You're very sensitive. Cheers. The first today. What day is it?
What's the time? Is it still night?

BRIGGS

Yes.

HIRST

The same night? I was dreaming of a waterfall. No, no, of a
lake. I think it was . . just recently. Can you remember when I
went to bed? Was it daylight? It's good to go to sleep in the

late afternoon. After tea and toast. You hear the faint beginnings of the evening sounds, and then nothing. Everywhere
else people are changing for dinner. You're tucked up, the
shutters closed, gaining a march on the world.

He passes his glass to BRIGGS, *who fills and returns it.*

Something is depressing me. What is it? It was the dream, yes.
Waterfalls. No, no, a lake. Water. Drowning. Not me. Someone else. How nice to have company. Can you imagine waking
up, finding no-one here, just furniture, staring at you? Most
unpleasant. I've known that condition, I've been through that
period – cheers – I came round to human beings in the end.
Like yourselves. A wise move. I tried laughing alone. Pathetic.
Have you all got drinks?

He looks at SPOONER.

Who's that? A friend of yours? Won't someone introduce me?

FOSTER
He's a friend of yours.

HIRST
In the past I knew remarkable people. I've a photograph album
somewhere. I'll find it. You'll be impressed by the faces. Very
handsome. Sitting on grass with hampers. I had a moustache.
Quite a few of my friends had moustaches. Remarkable faces.
Remarkable moustaches. What was it informed the scene?
A tenderness towards our fellows, perhaps. The sun shone. The
girls had lovely hair, dark, sometimes red. Under their dresses
their bodies were white. It's all in my album. I'll find it. You'll
be struck by the charm of the girls, their grace, the ease with
which they sit, pour tea, loll. It's all in my album.

He empties glass, holds it up.

Who is the kindest among you?

BRIGGS *takes glass to cabinet.*

Thank you. What would I do without the two of you? I'd sit here forever, waiting for a stranger to fill up my glass. What would I do while I waited? Look through my album? Make plans for the future?

BRIGGS

(*Bringing glass.*) You'd crawl to the bottle and stuff it between your teeth.

HIRST

No. I drink with dignity.

He drinks, looks at SPOONER.

Who is this man? Do I know him?

FOSTER

He says he's a friend of yours.

HIRST

My true friends look out at me from my album. I had my world. I have it. Don't think now that it's gone I'll choose to sneer at it, to cast doubt on it, to wonder if it properly existed. No. We're talking of my youth, which can never leave me. No. It existed. It was solid, the people in it were solid, while . . . transformed by light, while being sensitive . . . to all the changing light.

When I stood my shadow fell upon her. She looked up. Give me the bottle. Give me the bottle.

BRIGGS *gives him the bottle. He drinks from it.*

It's gone. Did it exist? It's gone. It never existed. It remains.

I am sitting here forever.

How kind of you. I wish you'd tell me what the weather's like. I wish you'd damnwell tell me what night it is, this night or the next night or the other one, the night before last. Be frank. Is it the night before last?

Help yourselves. I hate drinking alone. There's too much solitary shittery.

What was it? Shadows. Brightness, through leaves. Gambolling. In the bushes. Young lovers. A fall of water. It was my dream. The lake. Who was drowning in my dream?

It was blinding. I remember it. I've forgotten. By all that's sacred and holy. The sounds stopped. It was freezing. There's a gap in me. I can't fill it. There's a flood running through me. I can't plug it. They're blotting me out. Who is doing it? I'm suffocating. It's a muff. A muff, perfumed. Someone is doing me to death.

She looked up. I was staggered. I had never seen anything so beautiful. That's all poison. We can't be expected to live like that.

I remember nothing. I'm sitting in this room. I see you all, every one of you. A sociable gathering. The dispositions are kindly.

Am I asleep? There's no water. No-one is drowning.

Yes, yes, come on, come on, come on, pipe up, speak up,
speak up, speak up, you're fucking me about, you bastards,
ghosts, long ghosts, you're making noises, I can hear you
humming, I wear a crisp blue shirt at the Ritz, I wear a crisp
blue shirt at the Ritz, I know him well, the wine waiter, Boris,
Boris, he's been there for years, blinding shadows, then a fall of
water –

SPOONER
It was I drowning in your dream.

HIRST *falls to the floor. They all go to him.*
FOSTER *turns to* SPOONER.

FOSTER

Bugger off.

BRIGGS *pulls* HIRST *up.* HIRST *wards him off.*

HIRST
Unhand me.

He stands erect. SPOONER *moves to him.*

SPOONER
He has grandchildren. As have I. As I have. We both have
fathered. We are of an age. I know his wants. Let me take his
arm. Respect our age. Come, I'll seat you.

He takes HIRST'S *arm and leads him to a chair.*

There's no pity in these people.

FOSTER
Christ.

SPOONER

I am your true friend. That is why your dream . . . was so
distressing. You saw me drowning in your dream. But have no
fear. I am not drowned.

FOSTER

Christ.

SPOONER

(*To* HIRST.) Would you like me to make you some coffee?

BRIGGS

He thinks he's a waiter in Amsterdam.

FOSTER

Service non compris.

BRIGGS

Whereas he's a pintpot attendant in The Bull's Head. And a
pisspot attendant as well.

FOSTER

Our host must have been in The Bull's Head tonight, where
he had an unfortunate encounter. (*To* SPOONER.) Hey scout, I
think there's been some kind of misunderstanding. You're not
in some shithouse down by the docks. You're in the home of a
man of means, of a man of achievement. Do you understand
me?

He turns to BRIGGS.

Why am I bothering? Tell me. Eh?

He turns back to SPOONER.

Listen chummybum. We protect this gentleman against corruption, against men of craft, against men of evil, we could
destroy you without a glance, we take care of this gentleman,
we do it out of love.

He turns to BRIGGS.

Why am I talking to him? I'm wasting my time with a non-
starter. I must be going mad. I don't usually talk. I don't have
to. Normally I keep quiet.

He turns back to SPOONER.

I know what it is. There's something about you fascinates me.

SPOONER
It's my bearing.

FOSTER
That's what it must be.

BRIGGS
I've seen Irishmen chop his balls off.

FOSTER
I suppose once you've had Irishmen you've had everything.
(*To* SPOONER.) Listen. Keep it tidy. You follow? You've just
laid your hands on a rich and powerful man. It's not what
you're used to, scout. How can I make it clear? This is another
class. It's another realm of operation. It's a world of silk.
It's a world of organdie. It's a world of flower arrangements.
It's a world of eighteenth century cookery books. It's nothing
to do with toffeeapples and a packet of crisps. It's milk in the
bath. It's the cloth bellpull. It's organisation.

BRIGGS

It's not rubbish.

FOSTER

It's not rubbish. We deal in originals. Nothing duff, nothing ersatz, we don't open any old bottle of brandy. Mind you don't fall into a quicksand. (*To* BRIGGS.) Why don't I kick his head off and have done with it?

SPOONER

I'm the same age as your master. I used to picnic in the country too, at the same time as he.

FOSTER

Listen, my friend. This man in this chair, he's a creative man. He's an artist. We make life possible for him. We're in a position of trust. Don't try to drive a wedge into a happy household. You understand me? Don't try to make a nonsense out of family life.

BRIGGS

(*To* FOSTER.) If you can't, I can.

He moves to SPOONER *and beckons to him, with his forefinger.*

BRIGGS

Come here.

HIRST

Where are the sandwiches? Cut the bread.

BRIGGS

It's cut.

HIRST

It is not cut. Cut it!

BRIGGS *stands still.*

BRIGGS

I'll go and cut it.

He leaves the room.

HIRST

(*To* SPOONER.) I know you from somewhere.

FOSTER

I must clean the house. No-one else'll do it. Your financial adviser is coming to breakfast. I've got to think about that. His taste changes from day to day. One day he wants boiled eggs and toast, the next day orange juice and poached eggs, the next scrambled eggs and smoked salmon, the next a mushroom omelette and champagne. Any minute now it'll be dawn. A new day. Your financial adviser's dreaming of his breakfast. He's dreaming of eggs. Eggs, eggs. What kind of eggs? I'm exhausted. I've been up all night. But it never stops. Nothing stops. It's all fizz. This is my life. I have my brief arousals. They leave me panting. I can't take the pace in London. Nobody knows what I miss.

BRIGGS *enters and stands, listening.*

I miss the Siamese girls. I miss the girls in Bali. You don't come across them over here. You see them occasionally, on the steps of language schools, they're learning English, they're not prepared to have a giggle and a cuddle in their own language. Not in Regent street. A giggle and a cuddle. Sometimes

my ambitions extend no further than that. I could do something else. I could make another life. I don't have to waste my
time looking after a pisshound. I could find the right niche and
be happy. The right niche, the right happiness.

BRIGGS

We're out of bread. I'm looking at the housekeeper. Neurotic
poof. He prefers idleness. Unspeakable ponce. He prefers the
Malay Straits, where they give you hot toddy in a fourposter.
He's nothing but a vagabond cock. (*To* SPOONER.) Move over.

SPOONER *moves out of his way.*

BRIGGS

(*To* HIRST.) Get up.

HIRST *slowly stands.* BRIGGS *leads him to the door.*

BRIGGS

(*To* HIRST.) Keep on the move. Don't look back.

HIRST

I know that man.

BRIGGS *leads* HIRST *out of the room.*

Silence

FOSTER

Do you know what I saw once in the desert, in the Australian
desert? A man walking along carrying two umbrellas. Two
umbrellas. In the outback.

Pause

SPOONER

Was it raining?

FOSTER

No. It was a beautiful day. I nearly asked him what he was up
to but I changed my mind.

SPOONER

Why?

FOSTER

Well, I decided he must be some kind of lunatic. I thought he
would only confuse me.

FOSTER *walks about the room, stops at the door.*

Listen. You know what it's like when you're in a room with the
light on and then suddenly the light goes out? I'll show you.
It's like this.

He turns the light out.

BLACKOUT

ACT TWO

Morning

SPOONER *is alone in the room. The curtains are still closed, but shafts of light enter the room.*

He is sitting.

He stands, goes slowly to door, tries handle, with fatigue, withdraws.

SPOONER
I have known this before. Morning. A locked door. A house of silence and strangers.

He sits, shivers.

The door is unlocked. BRIGGS *comes in, key in hand. He is wearing a suit. He opens the curtains. Daylight.*

BRIGGS
I've been asked to inquire if you're hungry.

SPOONER
Food? I never touch it.

BRIGGS
The financial adviser didn't turn up. You can have his breakfast. He phoned his order through, then phoned again to cancel the appointment.

SPOONER
For what reason?

BRIGGS

Jack spoke to him, not me.

SPOONER

What reason did he give your friend?

BRIGGS

Jack said he said he found himself without warning in the centre of a vast aboriginal financial calamity.

Pause

SPOONER

He clearly needs an adviser.

Pause

BRIGGS

I won't bring you breakfast if you're going to waste it.

SPOONER

I abhor waste.

BRIGGS *goes out.*

I have known this before. The door unlocked. The entrance of a stranger. The offer of alms. The shark in the harbour.

Silence

BRIGGS *enters carrying a tray. On the tray are breakfast dishes covered by silver lids and a bottle of champagne in a bucket.*

He places the tray on a small table and brings a chair to the table.

BRIGGS

Scrambled eggs. Shall I open the champagne?

SPOONER

Is it cold?

BRIGGS

Freezing.

SPOONER

Please open it.

BRIGGS *begins to open bottle.* **SPOONER** *lifts lids, peers, sets lids aside, butters toast.*

SPOONER

Who is the cook?

BRIGGS

We share all burdens, Jack and myself.

BRIGGS *pours champagne. Offers glass.* **SPOONER** *sips.*

Pause

SPOONER

Thank you.

SPOONER *begins to eat.* **BRIGGS** *draws up a chair to the table and sits, watching.*

BRIGGS

We're old friends, Jack and myself. We met at a street corner.
I should tell you he'll deny this account. His story will be
different. I was standing at a street corner. A car drew up. It
was him. He asked me the way to Bolsover street. I told him
Bolsover street was in the middle of an intricate one-way system. It was a one-way system easy enough to get into. The
only trouble was that, once in, you couldn't get out. I told him
his best bet, if he really wanted to get to Bolsover street, was to
take the first left, first right, second right, third on the left,
keep his eye open for a hardware shop, go right round the
square, keeping to the inside lane, take the second Mews on the
right and then stop. He will find himself facing a very tall
office block, with a crescent courtyard. He can take advantage
of this office block. He can go round the crescent, come out the
other way, follow the arrows, go past two sets of traffic lights
and take the next left indicated by the first green filter he
comes across. He's got the Post Office Tower in his vision the
whole time. All he's got to do is to reverse into the underground car park, change gear, go straight on, and he'll find
himself in Bolsover street with no trouble at all. I did warn
him, though, that he'll still be faced with the problem, having
found Bolsover street, of losing it. I told him I knew one or two
people who'd been wandering up and down Bolsover street for
years. They'd wasted their bloody youth there. The people
who live there, their faces are grey, they're in a state of despair,
but nobody pays any attention, you see. All people are worried
about is their illgotten gains. I wrote to The Times about it.
Life At A Dead End, I called it. Went for nothing. Anyway,
I told him that probably the best thing he could do was to
forget the whole idea of getting to Bolsover street. I remember
saying to him: This trip you've got in mind, drop it, it could
prove fatal. But he said he had to deliver a parcel. Anyway, I
took all this trouble with him because he had a nice open face.

He looked like a man who would always do good to others
himself. Normally I wouldn't give a fuck. I should tell you
he'll deny this account. His story will be different.

SPOONER *places the lid on his plate.*

BRIGGS *pours champagne into* SPOONER's *glass.*

When did you last have champagne for breakfast?

SPOONER

Well, to be quite honest, I'm a champagne drinker.

BRIGGS

Oh, are you?

SPOONER

I know my wines. (*He drinks.*) Dijon. In the thirties. I made
many trips to Dijon, for the winetasting, with my French
translator. Even after his death, I continued to go to Dijon,
until I could go no longer.

Pause

Hugo. A good companion.

Pause.

You will wonder of course what he translated. The answer is
my verse. I am a poet.

Pause

BRIGGS

I thought poets were young.

SPOONER

I am young. (*He reaches for the bottle.*) Can I help you to a glass?

BRIGGS

No, thank you.

SPOONER *examines the bottle.*

SPOONER

An excellent choice.

BRIGGS

Not mine.

SPOONER

(*Pouring.*) Translating verse is an extremely difficult task. Only the Rumanians remain respectable exponents of the craft.

BRIGGS

Bit early in the morning for all this, isn't it?

SPOONER *drinks.*

Finish the bottle. Doctor's orders.

SPOONER

Can I enquire as to why I was locked in this room, by the way?

BRIGGS

Doctor's orders.

Pause

Tell me when you're ready for coffee.

Pause

It must be wonderful to be a poet and to have admirers. And translators. And to be young. I'm neither one nor the other.

SPOONER
Yes. You've reminded me. I must be off. I have a meeting at twelve. Thank you so much for breakfast.

BRIGGS
What meeting?

SPOONER
A board meeting. I'm on the board of a recently inaugurated poetry magazine. We have our first meeting at twelve. Can't be late.

BRIGGS
Where's the meeting?

SPOONER
At The Bull's Head in Chalk Farm. The landlord is kindly allowing us the use of a private room on the first floor. It is essential that the meeting be private, you see, as we shall be discussing policy.

BRIGGS
The Bull's Head in Chalk Farm?

SPOONER
Yes. The landlord is a friend of mine. It is on that account that he has favoured us with a private room. It is true of course that I informed him Lord Lancer would be attending the

meeting. He at once appreciated that a certain degree of sequesteredness would be the order of the day.

BRIGGS

Lord Lancer?

SPOONER

Our patron.

BRIGGS

He's not one of the Bengal Lancers, is he?

SPOONER

No, no. He's of Norman descent.

BRIGGS

A man of culture?

SPOONER

Impeccable credentials.

BRIGGS

Some of these aristocrats hate the arts.

SPOONER

Lord Lancer is a man of honour. He loves the arts. He has declared this love in public. He never goes back on his word. But I must be off. Lord Lancer does not subscribe to the view that poets can treat time with nonchalance.

BRIGGS

Jack could do with a patron.

SPOONER

Jack?

BRIGGS

He's a poet.

SPOONER

A poet? Really? Well, if he'd like to send me some examples of
his work, double spaced on quarto, with copies in a separate
folder by separate post in case of loss or misappropriation,
stamped addressed envelope enclosed, I'll read them.

BRIGGS

That's very nice of you.

SPOONER

Not at all. You can tell him he can look forward to a scrupulously honest and, if I may say so, highly sensitive judgement.

BRIGGS

I'll tell him. He's in real need of a patron. The boss could be
his patron, but he's not interested. Perhaps because he's a poet
himself. It's possible there's an element of jealousy in it, I
don't know. Not that the boss isn't a very kind man. He is.
He's a very civilised man. But he's still human.

Pause

SPOONER

The boss . . . is a poet himself?

BRIGGS

Don't be silly. He's more than that, isn't he? He's an essayist
and critic as well. He's a man of letters.

SPOONER

I thought his face was familiar.

The telephone buzzes. BRIGGS *goes to it, lifts it, listens.*

BRIGGS
Yes, sir.

BRIGGS *picks up the tray and takes it out.*

SPOONER *sits still.*

SPOONER
I have known this before. The voice unheard. A listener.
The command from an upper floor.

He pours champagne.

HIRST *enters, wearing a suit, followed by* BRIGGS.

HIRST
Charles. How nice of you to drop in.

He shakes SPOONER's *hand.*

Have they been looking after you all right? Denson, let's have
some coffee.

BRIGGS *leaves the room.*

You're looking remarkably well. Haven't changed a bit. It's
the squash, I expect. Keeps you up to the mark. You were
quite a dab hand at Oxford, as I remember. Still at it? Wise
man. Sensible chap. My goodness, it's years. When did we last
meet? I have a suspicion we last dined together in '38, at the
club. Does that accord with your recollection? Croxley was
there, yes, Wyatt, it all comes back to me, Burston-Smith.

What a bunch. What a night, as I recall. All dead now, of course. No, no! I'm a fool. I'm an idiot. Our last encounter – I remember it well. Pavilion at Lord's in '39, against the West Indies, Hutton and Compton batting superbly, Constantine bowling, war looming. Surely I'm right? We shared a particularly fine bottle of port. You look as fit now as you did then. Did you have a good war?

BRIGGS *comes in with coffee, places it on table.*

Oh thank you, Denson. Leave it there, will you? That will do.

BRIGGS *leaves the room.*

How's Emily? What a woman. (*Pouring.*) Black? Here you are. What a woman. Have to tell you I fell in love with her once upon a time. Have to confess it to you. Took her out to tea, in Dorchester. Told her of my yearning. Decided to take the bull by the horns. Proposed that she betray you. Admitted you were a damn fine chap, but pointed out I would be taking nothing that belonged to you, simply that portion of herself all women keep in reserve, for a rainy day. Had an infernal job persuading her. Said she adored you, her life would be meaningless were she to be false. Plied her with buttered scones, Wiltshire cream, crumpets and strawberries. Eventually she succumbed. Don't suppose you ever knew about it, what? Oh, we're too old now for it to matter, don't you agree?

He sits, with coffee.

I rented a little cottage for the summer. She used to motor to me twice or thrice a week. I was an integral part of her shopping expeditions. You were both living on the farm then. That's right. Her father's farm. She would come to me at tea-time, or at coffee-time, the innocent hours. That summer she was mine, while you imagined her to be solely yours.

He sips the coffee.

She loved the cottage. She loved the flowers. As did I. Narcissi, crocus, dog's tooth violets, fuchsia, jonquils, pinks, verbena.

Pause

Her delicate hands.

Pause

I'll never forget her way with jonquils.

Pause

Do you remember once, was it in '37, you took her to France? I was on the same boat. Kept to my cabin. While you were doing your exercises she came to me. Her ardour was, in my experience, unparalleled. Ah well.

Pause

You were always preoccupied with your physical . . condition . . weren't you? Don't blame you. Damn fine figure of a chap. Natural athlete. Medals, scrolls, your name inscribed in gold. Once a man has breasted the tape, alone, he is breasting the tape forever. His golden moment can never be tarnished. Do you run still? Why was it we saw so little of each other, after we came down from Oxford? I mean, you had another string to your bow, did you not? You were a literary man. As was I. Yes, yes, I know we shared the occasional picnic, with Tubby Wells and all that crowd, we shared the occasional whisky and soda at the club, but we were never close, were we? I wonder why. Of course I was successful awfully early.

Pause

You did say you had a good war, didn't you?

SPOONER

A rather good one, yes.

HIRST

How splendid. The RAF?

SPOONER

The Navy.

HIRST

How splendid. Destroyers?

SPOONER

Torpedo boats.

HIRST

First rate. Kill any Germans?

SPOONER

One or two.

HIRST

Well done.

SPOONER

And you?

HIRST

I was in Military Intelligence.

SPOONER

Ah.

Pause

HIRST

You pursued your literary career, after the war?

SPOONER

Oh yes.

HIRST

So did I.

SPOONER

I believe you've done rather well.

HIRST

Oh quite well, yes. Past my best now.

SPOONER

Do you ever see Stella?

Pause

HIRST

Stella?

SPOONER

You can't have forgotten.

HIRST

Stella who?

SPOONER

Stella Winstanley.

HIRST

Winstanley?

SPOONER

Bunty Winstanley's sister.

HIRST

Oh, Bunty. No, I never see her.

SPOONER

You were rather taken with her.

HIRST

Was I, old chap? How did you know?

SPOONER

I was terribly fond of Bunty. He was most dreadfully annoyed
with you. Wanted to punch you on the nose.

HIRST

What for?

SPOONER

For seducing his sister.

HIRST

What business was it of his?

SPOONER

He was her brother.

HIRST

That's my point.

Pause

What on earth are you driving at?

SPOONER

Bunty introduced Rupert to Stella. He was very fond of Rupert. He gave the bride away. He and Rupert were terribly old friends. He threatened to horsewhip you.

HIRST

Who did?

SPOONER

Bunty.

HIRST

He never had the guts to speak to me himself.

SPOONER

Stella begged him not to. She implored him to stay his hand. She implored him not to tell Rupert.

HIRST

I see. But who told Bunty?

SPOONER

I told Bunty. I was frightfully fond of Bunty. I was also frightfully fond of Stella.

Pause

HIRST

You appear to have been a close friend of the family.

SPOONER

Mainly of Arabella's. We used to ride together.

HIRST

Arabella Hinscott?

SPOONER

Yes.

HIRST

I knew her at Oxford.

SPOONER

So did I.

HIRST

I was very fond of Arabella.

SPOONER

Arabella was very fond of me. Bunty was never sure of precisely how fond she was of me, nor of what form her fondness took.

HIRST

What in God's name do you mean?

SPOONER

Bunty trusted me. I was best man at their wedding. He also trusted Arabella.

HIRST

I should warn you that I was always extremely fond of Arabella. Her father was my tutor. I used to stay at their house.

SPOONER

I knew her father well. He took a great interest in me.

HIRST

Arabella was a girl of the most refined and organised sensibilities.

SPOONER

I agree.

Pause

HIRST

Are you trying to tell me that you had an affair with Arabella?

SPOONER

A form of an affair. She had no wish for full consummation. She was content with her particular predilection. Consuming the male member.

HIRST *stands.*

HIRST

I'm beginning to believe you're a scoundrel. How dare you speak of Arabella Hinscott in such a fashion? I'll have you blackballed from the club!

SPOONER

Oh my dear sir, may I remind you that you betrayed Stella Winstanley with Emily Spooner, my own wife, throughout a long and soiled summer, a fact known at the time throughout the Home Counties? May I further remind you that Muriel Blackwood and Doreen Busby have never recovered from your insane and corrosive sexual absolutism? May I further remind you that your friendship with and corruption of Geoffrey Ramsden at Oxford was the talk of Balliol and Christchurch Cathedral?

HIRST

This is scandalous! How dare you? I'll have you horse-whipped!

SPOONER

It is you, sir, who have behaved scandalously. To the fairest of sexes, of which my wife was the fairest representative. It is you who have behaved unnaturally and scandalously, to the woman who was joined to me in God.

HIRST

I, sir? Unnaturally? Scandalously?

SPOONER

Scandalously. She told me all.

HIRST

You listen to the drivellings of a farmer's wife?

SPOONER

Since I was the farmer, yes.

HIRST

You were no farmer, sir. A weekend wanker.

SPOONER

I wrote my Homage to Wessex in the summerhouse at West Upfield.

HIRST

I have never had the good fortune to read it.

SPOONER

It is written in terza rima, a form which, if you will forgive my saying so, you have never been able to master.

HIRST

This is outrageous! Who are you? What are you doing in my house?

He goes to the door and calls.

Denson! A whisky and soda!

He walks about the room.

You are clearly a lout. The Charles Wetherby I knew was a gentleman. I see a figure reduced. I am sorry for you. Where is the moral ardour that sustained you once? Gone down the hatch.

BRIGGS *enters, pours whisky and soda, gives it to* HIRST. HIRST *looks at it.*

Down the hatch. Right down the hatch. (*He drinks.*) I do not understand . . . I do not understand . . . and I see it all about me . . . continually . . . how the most sensitive and cultivated of men can so easily change, almost overnight, into the bully, the cutpurse, the brigand. In my day nobody changed. A man was. Only religion could alter him, and that at least was a glorious misery.

He drinks, and sits in his chair.

We are not banditti here. I am prepared to be patient. I shall be kind to you. I shall show you my library. I might even show you my study. I might even show you my pen, and my blottingpad. I might even show you my footstool.

He holds out his glass.

Another.

BRIGGS *takes glass, fills it, returns it.*

I might even show you my photograph album. You might even
see a face in it which might remind you of your own, of what
you once were. You might see faces of others, in shadow, or
cheeks of others, turning, or jaws, or backs of necks, or eyes,
dark under hats, which might remind you of others, whom
once you knew, whom you thought long dead, but from whom
you will still receive a sidelong glance, if you can face the good
ghost. Allow the love of the good ghost. They possess all that
emotion . . . trapped. Bow to it. It will assuredly never release
them, but who knows . . . what relief . . . it may give to
them . . . who knows how they may quicken . . . in their chains,
in their glass jars. You think it cruel . . . to quicken them, when
they are fixed, imprisoned? No . . no. Deeply, deeply, they
wish to respond to your touch, to your look, and when you
smile, their joy . . . is unbounded. And so I say to you, tender
the dead, as you would yourself be tendered, now, in what you
would describe as your life.

He drinks.

BRIGGS
They're blank, mate, blank. The blank dead.

Silence

HIRST
Nonsense.

Pause

Pass the bottle.

BRIGGS

No.

HIRST

What?

BRIGGS

I said no.

HIRST

No pranks. No mischief. Give me the bottle.

Pause

BRIGGS

I've refused.

HIRST

Refusal can lead to dismissal.

BRIGGS

You can't dismiss me.

HIRST

Why not?

BRIGGS

Because I won't go.

HIRST

If I tell you to go, you will go. Give me the bottle.

Silence

HIRST *turns to* SPOONER.

HIRST

Bring me the bottle.

SPOONER *goes to cabinet.* BRIGGS *does not move.*
SPOONER *picks up whisky bottle, takes it to* HIRST.
HIRST *pours and places bottle at his side.*

BRIGGS

I'll have one myself.

BRIGGS *takes a glass to the bottle, pours and drinks.*

HIRST

What impertinence. Well, it doesn't matter. He was always a
scallywag. Is it raining? It so often rains, in August, in England.
Do you ever examine the gullies of the English countryside?
Under the twigs, under the dead leaves, you'll find tennis balls,
blackened. Girls threw them for their dogs, or children, for
each other, they rolled into the gully. They are lost there, given
up for dead, centuries old.

FOSTER *comes into the room.*

FOSTER

It's time for your morning walk.

Pause

I said it's time for your morning walk.

HIRST

My morning walk? No, no, I'm afraid I don't have the time
this morning.

FOSTER

It's time for your walk across the Heath.

HIRST

I can't possibly. I'm too busy. I have too many things to do.

FOSTER

What's that you're drinking?

SPOONER

The great malt which wounds.

HIRST

(*To* SPOONER.) My God, you haven't got a drink. Where's your glass?

SPOONER

Thank you. It would be unwise to mix my drinks.

HIRST

Mix?

SPOONER

I was drinking champagne.

HIRST

Of course you were, of course. Albert, another bottle.

BRIGGS

Certainly, sir.

BRIGGS *goes out*.

HIRST

I can't possibly. I have too many things to do. I have an essay to write. A critical essay. We'll have to check the files, find out what it is I'm supposed to be appraising. At the moment it's slipped my mind.

SPOONER

I could help you there.

HIRST

Oh?

SPOONER

On two counts. Firstly, I have the nose of a ferret. I can find anything in a file. Secondly, I have written any number of critical essays myself. Do you actually have a secretary?

FOSTER

I'm his secretary.

SPOONER

A secretarial post does less than justice to your talents. A young poet should travel. Travel and suffer. Join the navy, perhaps, and see the sea. Voyage and explore.

FOSTER

I've sailored. I've been there and back. I'm here where I'm needed.

BRIGGS *enters with champagne, stops at door, listens.*

SPOONER

(*To* HIRST.) You mentioned a photograph album. I could go through it with you. I could put names to the faces. A proper exhumation could take place. Yes, I am confident that I could be of enormous aid in that area.

FOSTER

Those faces are nameless, friend.

BRIGGS *comes into room, sets down champagne bucket.*

BRIGGS

And they'll always be nameless.

HIRST

There are places in my heart . . . where no living soul . . . has . . . or can ever . . . trespass.

BRIGGS *opens champagne, pours glass for* SPOONER.

BRIGGS

Here you are. Fresh as a daisy. (*To* HIRST.) A drop for you, sir?

HIRST

No, no. I'll stay . . . where I am.

BRIGGS

I'll join Mr. Friend, if I may, sir?

HIRST

Naturally.

BRIGGS

(*To* FOSTER.) Where's your glass?

FOSTER

No thanks.

HIRST

Oh come on, be sociable. Be sociable. Consort with the society
to which you're attached. To which you're attached as if by
bonds of steel. Mingle.

BRIGGS *pours a glass for* FOSTER.

FOSTER

It isn't even lunchtime.

BRIGGS

The best time to drink champagne is before lunch, you cunt.

FOSTER

Don't call me a cunt.

HIRST

We three, never forget, are the oldest of friends.

BRIGGS

That's why I called him a cunt.

FOSTER

(*To* BRIGGS.) Stop talking.

HIRST *lifts his glass.*

HIRST

To our good fortune.

Mutters of 'Cheers'. They all drink.
HIRST *looks at the window.*

HIRST

The light . . . out there . . . is gloomy . . . hardly daylight at all.
It is falling, rapidly. Distasteful. Let us close the curtains. Put
the lamps on.

BRIGGS *closes the curtains, lights lamps.*

HIRST

Ah. What relief.

Pause

How happy it is.

Pause

Today I shall come to a conclusion. There are certain matters
. . . which today I shall resolve.

SPOONER

I'll help you.

FOSTER

I was in Bali when they sent for me. I didn't have to leave, I
didn't have to come here. But I felt I was . . . called . . . I had
no alternative. I didn't have to leave that beautiful isle. But I
was intrigued. I was only a boy. But I was nondescript and
anonymous. A famous writer wanted me. He wanted me to be
his secretary, his chauffeur, his housekeeper, his amanuensis.
How did he know of me? Who told him?

SPOONER

He made an imaginative leap. Few can do it. Few do it. He did
it. And that's why God loves him.

BRIGGS

You came on my recommendation. I've always liked youth
because you can use it. But it has to be open and honest. If it
isn't open and honest you can't use it. I recommended you.
You were open, the whole world before you.

FOSTER

I find the work fruitful. I'm in touch with a very special
intelligence. This intelligence I find nourishing. I have been
nourished by it. It's enlarged me. Therefore it's an intelligence
worth serving. I find its demands natural. Not only that.
They're legal. I'm not doing anything crooked. It's a relief.
I could so easily have been bent. I have a sense of dignity in my
work, a sense of honour. It never leaves me. Of service to a
cause.

He refers to BRIGGS.

He is my associate. He was my proposer. I've learnt a great
deal from him. He's been my guide. The most unselfish
person I've ever met. He'll tell you. Let him speak.

BRIGGS

Who to?

FOSTER

What?

BRIGGS

Speak? Who to?

FOSTER *looks at* SPOONER.

FOSTER

To . . . him.

BRIGGS

To him? To a pisshole collector? To a shithouse operator?
To a jamrag vendor? What the fuck are you talking about?
Look at him. He's a mingejuice bottler, a fucking shitcake
baker. What are you talking to him for?

HIRST

Yes, yes, but he's a good man at heart. I knew him at Oxford.

Silence

SPOONER

(*To* HIRST.) Let me live with you and be your secretary.

HIRST

Is there a big fly in here? I hear buzzing.

SPOONER

No.

HIRST

You say no.

SPOONER

Yes.

Pause

I ask you . . . to consider me for the post. If I were wearing a
suit such as your own you would see me in a different light. I'm
extremely good with tradespeople, hawkers, canvassers, nuns.
I can be silent when desired or, when desired, convivial. I can
discuss any subject of your choice – the future of the country,
wild flowers, the Olympic Games. It is true I have fallen on

hard times, but my imagination and intelligence are unimpaired. My will to work has not been eroded. I remain capable of undertaking the gravest and most daunting responsibilities. Temperamentally I can be what you wish. My character is, at core, a humble one. I am an honest man and, moreover, I am not too old to learn. My cooking is not to be sneezed at. I lean towards French cuisine but food without frills is not beyond my competency. I have a keen eye for dust. My kitchen would be immaculate. I am tender towards objects. I would take good care of your silver. I play chess, billiards, and the piano. I could play Chopin for you. I could read the Bible to you. I am a good companion.

Pause

My career, I admit it freely, has been chequered. I was one of the golden of my generation. Something happened. I don't know what it was. Nevertheless I am I and have survived insult and deprivation. I am I. I offer myself not abjectly but with ancient pride. I come to you as a warrior. I shall be happy to serve you as my master. I bend my knee to your excellence. I am furnished with the qualities of piety, prudence, liberality and goodness. Decline them at your peril. It is my task as a gentleman to remain amiable in my behaviour, courageous in my undertakings, discreet and gallant in my executions, by which I mean your private life would remain your own. However, I shall be sensible to the least wrong offered you. My sword shall be ready to dissever all manifest embodiments of malign forces that conspire to your ruin. I shall regard it as incumbent upon me to preserve a clear countenance and a clean conscience. I will accept death's challenge on your behalf. I shall meet it, for your sake, boldly, whether it be in the field or in the bedchamber. I am your Chevalier. I had rather bury myself in a tomb of honour than permit your dignity to be sullied by domestic enemy or foreign foe. I am yours to command.

Silence

HIRST *is still, sitting.*
FOSTER *and* BRIGGS *are still, standing.*

SPOONER

Before you reply, I would like to say one thing more. I occasionally organise poetry readings, in the upstairs room of a particular public house. They are reasonably well attended, mainly by the young. I would be happy to offer you an evening of your own. You could read your own work, to an interested and informed audience, to an audience brimming over with potential for the greatest possible enthusiasm. I can guarantee a full house, and I will be happy to arrange a straightforward fee for you or, if you prefer, a substantial share of the profits. The young, I can assure you, would flock to hear you. My committee would deem it a singular honour to act as your host. You would be introduced by an authority on your work, perhaps myself. After the reading, which I am confident will be a remarkable success, we could repair to the bar below, where the landlord – who happens to be a friend of mine – would I know be overjoyed to entertain you, with the compliments of the house. Nearby is an Indian restaurant of excellent standing, at which you would be the guest of my committee. Your face is so seldom seen, your words, known to so many, have been so seldom heard, in the absolute authority of your own rendering, that this event would qualify for that rarest of categories: the unique. I beg you to consider seriously the social implications of such an adventure. You would be there in body. It would bring you to the young, the young to you. The elderly, also, those who have almost lost hope, would on this occasion leave their homes and present themselves. You would have no trouble with the press. I would take upon myself the charge of

keeping them from nuisance. Perhaps you might agree to half
a dozen photographs or so, but no more. Unless of course you
positively wished, on such an occasion, to speak. Unless you
preferred to hold, let us say, a small press conference, after the
reading, before supper, whereby you could speak through the
press to the world. But that is by the by, and would in no sense
be a condition. Let us content ourselves with the idea of an
intimate reading, in a pleasing and conducive environment, let
us consider an evening to be remembered, by all who take
part in her.

Silence

HIRST

Let us change the subject.

Pause

For the last time.

Pause

What have I said?

FOSTER

You said you're changing the subject for the last time.

HIRST

But what does that mean?

FOSTER

It means you'll never change the subject again.

HIRST

Never?

FOSTER
Never.

HIRST
Never?

FOSTER
You said for the last time.

HIRST
But what does that *mean*? What does it *mean*?

FOSTER
It means forever. It means that the subject is changed once and
for all and for the last time forever. If the subject is winter, for
instance, it'll be winter forever.

HIRST
Is the subject winter?

FOSTER
The subject is now winter. So it'll therefore be winter forever.

BRIGGS
And for the last time.

FOSTER
Which will last forever. If the subject is winter, for example,
spring will never come.

HIRST
But let me ask you – I must ask you –

FOSTER
Summer will never come.

BRIGGS

The trees –

FOSTER

Will never bud.

HIRST

I must ask you –

BRIGGS

Snow –

FOSTER

Will fall forever. Because you've changed the subject. For the last time.

HIRST

But have we? That's my question. Have I? Have we changed the subject?

FOSTER

Of course. The previous subject is closed.

HIRST

What was the previous subject?

FOSTER

It's forgotten. You've changed it.

HIRST

What is the present subject?

FOSTER

That there is no possibility of changing the subject since the subject has now been changed.

BRIGGS

For the last time.

FOSTER

So that nothing else will happen forever. You'll simply be sitting here forever.

BRIGGS

But not alone.

FOSTER

No. We'll be with you. Briggs and me.

Pause

HIRST

It's night.

FOSTER

And will always be night.

BRIGGS

Because the subject –

FOSTER

Can never be changed.

Silence

HIRST

But I hear sounds of birds. Don't you hear them? Sounds I never heard before. I hear them as they must have sounded

ff

Contemporary Classics

'Faber is well known for its drama output, but its new series of collected plays, *Contemporary Classics*, is particularly worth owning because of both the content and the chic look of the books. Featured authors represent a who's who of contemporary theatre and all are primarily masters of the verbal art. *Highly recommended.*' Steve Grant, **Time Out**

Alan Ayckbourn: Plays One
Alan Bennett: Plays One
Steven Berkoff:
Plays One and Plays Two
Brian Friel: Plays One
Trevor Griffiths: Plays One
Christopher Hampton: Plays One
David Hare:
Plays One and Plays Two
Tony Harrison: Plays Three
Ronald Harwood: Plays Two
Sharman Macdonald: Plays One
Frank McGuinness: Plays One
John Osborne: Plays One
Harold Pinter:
Plays One, Plays Two, Plays Three and Plays Four
Sam Shepard: Plays Two
Wallace Shawn: Plays One
Tom Stoppard:
Plays One and Plays Two
Nick Ward: Plays One
Timberlake Wertenbaker: Plays One

then, when I was young, although I never heard them then, although they sounded about us then.

Pause

Yes. It is true. I am walking towards a lake. Someone is following me, through the trees. I lose him, easily. I see a body in the water, floating. I am excited. I look closer and see I was mistaken. There is nothing in the water. I say to myself, I saw a body, drowning. But I am mistaken. There is nothing there.

Silence

SPOONER

No. You are in no man's land. Which never moves, which never changes, which never grows older, but which remains forever, icy and silent.

Silence

HIRST

I'll drink to that.

He drinks.

SLOW FADE